52 Instant
Skits

Paul McCusker has over 40 published works,
including plays, novels, screenplays, radio
dramas and lyrics. He is the writer and director
of the Peabody Award-winning radio drama
Dietrich Bonhoeffer: The Cost of Freedom.
Paul lives in Colorado Springs with his wife
Elizabeth and two children.

Dedication

To Elizabeth, Tommy and Ellie —
who always sacrifice more than I do when I write.

Other works by the author

NOVELS:
You Say Tomato (with Adrian Plass)
Epiphany
Catacombs
The Faded Flower

GENERAL RESOURCE:
52 Quick Sketches
The Ultimate Youth Drama Book
Playwriting: A Study In Choices &
    Challenges

PLAYS:
The Case Of The Frozen Saints
The First Church Of Pete's Garage
The Revised Standard Version
    Of Jack Hill
Dear Diary
Camp W
Catacombs
Death By Chocolate
Family Outings
Pap's Place

MUSICALS:
The Meaning Of Life & Other Vanities
    (with Tim Albritton)
Shine The Light Of Christmas (with
    Dave and Jan Williamson)
A Time For Christmas (with David
    Clydesdale, Steve Amerson,
    Lowell Alexander)

**ADVENTURES IN ODYSSEY
    NOVELS:**
Strange Journey Back
High Flyer With A Flat Tire
Secret Cave of Robin Wood
Behind The Locked Door
Lights Out At Camp What-A-Nut
The King's Quest
Danger Lies Ahead
Point of No Return
Dark Passage
Freedom Run
Stranger's Message
Carnival of Secrets

VIDEOS:
Adventures In Odyssey: Once Upon
    An Avalanche
Adventures In Odyssey: Go
    West, Young Man

PASSAGES NOVELS:
Passages 1: Darien's Rise
Passages 2: Arin's Judgement
Passages 3: Annison's Risk
Passages 4: Glennall's Betrayal
Passages 5: Draven's Defiance
Passages 6: Fendar's Legacy

52 Instant Skits

Paul McCusker

MONARCH
BOOKS

Mill Hill, London, and Grand Rapids, Michigan

First published in 2003 by
Monarch Books, Concorde House,
Grenville Place, Mill Hill, London NW7 3SA.

ISBN 1 85424 633 X (UK)
ISBN 0 8254 6230 4 (USA)

Distributed by:
UK: STL, PO Box 300, Kingstown Broadway, Carlisle,
Cumbria CA3 0QS;
USA: Kregel Publications, PO Box 2607,
Grand Rapids, Michigan 49501.

British Library Cataloguing in Publication Data

A catalogue record for this book is
available from the British Library.

Designed and produced by
Gazelle Creative Productions Ltd, Concorde House, Grenville
Place, Mill Hill, London NW7 3SA

Contents

Introduction   7
 1. Avoiding accountability   9
 2. Family boycott   14
 3. Academics   19
 4. Clichés   23
 5. Exegetical explanations   26
 6. Len's birthday   28
 7. Nice   34
 8. Men of God   39
 9. Too nice   45
10. In the ghetto   49
11. Unity   55
12. A case of communication   59
13. Formulas   68
14. Revelation   71
15. Pre-emptive strike   77
16. On the motorway   82
17. Church splits   88
18. Interview with an old man   93
19. Interview with an old woman   99
20. The woman at the well   105
21. Going to church   110
22. Whose music?   114
23. Giving   117
24. The retirement   122
25. Healing   126
26. God told me   130
27. Life on the Box   134
28. Too many programmes, too many courses   137

Contents

29. The calling   140

30. The chair   143

31. Honestly   146

32. So... what's wrong with it?   149

33. The mid-life crisis   153

34. Protection   162

35. Dramatic conversions   166

36. Instant Christianity   171

37. The date   174

38. The marathon runners (a parable)   179

39. The hypochondriac   184

40. Executive decisions   189

41. Promises   193

42. The coat of many needles   196

43. Quite a surprise   202

44. The family room   206

45. Busy mum   210

46. The secret   218

47. War wear   224

48. Lunch in the park   229

49. The nice creed   235

50. Therapy   240

51. The test drive   247

52. Worship   253

Introduction

52 Instant Skits is, in part, an answer to the question: Where can I find something fun, thought-provoking, quick to rehearse and easy to perform? The sketches in this collection were written to fit the bill. They're designed to be easy-to-use in just about any setting or venue where you'd like to entertain, stimulate discussion, or merely to give an audience something to think about.

Versatility is also a goal here. The settings and subsequent sets can be as simple or as elaborate as you want to make them. Rehearsal time is completely at your discretion — spend a few minutes, a few days or even a few weeks, that's up to you.

The sketches cover a variety of topics through a variety of approaches. Each one has a theme attached to help you find the sketch you may be looking for, but the themes are broad and the sketches encompass one aspect of each theme. (For example, it's safe to say we could have written 52 sketches on friendship or relationship alone!) The styles are also varied, allowing room for straight drama, comedy, absurd wordplay, slapstick, monologues and reader's theatre.

In most cases, you can use whatever gender is appropriate or available. Many are written to be played by either. We've also had to acknowledge that these sketches will be used on both sides of the Atlantic, so I've "translated" various unfamiliar words or phrases in [brackets]. Or, in some cases, a different version of the sketch has been created altogether. One sketch in this collection wreaks havoc on the words and phrases of both countries and won't include a "translation" for obvious reasons.

A few hints about terminology. *Beats* are changes in the timing or flow of the dialogue, allowing for a new thought or change of subject. *Pause* is traditionally longer than a *beat* and tends to be a momentary stop in the flow of dialogue which allows the character to think about, react to or take action. There are no hard-and-fast rules about the exact length of time a *beat* or a *pause* may last. It's whatever is appropriate to the character, dialogue and direction.

Because the sketches were written to be flexible to almost any location, I didn't include specifics about *stage left* or *stage right*. You'll have to figure those out, depending on where these sketches are being performed. I've only indicated stage instructions where they're necessary to understanding the sketch. You'll also notice that *curtain* and *blackout* are missing. How you end the sketch is up to you. In lieu of a traditional stage where the actors truly can get off and out of sight, you may want to have them "freeze" in place while you or the host or whoever is in charge takes the stage.

It's our hope that these sketches will be stimulating and fun, true team-builders and enjoyable for your audience. Your suggestions and comments for future collections are also welcome.

Paul McCusker
2003

1. **Avoiding accountability**

THEME
Accountability.

SITUATION
Five characters instruct us – in Reader's Theatre style – how to avoid accountability in our lives.

CHARACTERS
Reader One
Reader Two
Reader Three
Reader Four
Reader Five

PLACE
Anywhere.

━━━
SKIT

[Stools for everyone. They enter, carrying Reader's Theatre folders in the grand Reader's Theatre tradition. They are wearing black turtlenecks. They sit down with precise coordination and begin...]

ALL   Avoiding Accountability.

ONE   A primer.

TWO   A necessity for living as Christians in this modern world of –

ALL   Rationalizations.

THREE   For accountability is a process in which we are provoked to do what is acceptable to Him –

FOUR   – and to expect correction when do those things that are *not* acceptable to Him.

ALL   Hebrews 10:24 and 25.

FIVE   "And let us consider how to stimulate

FOUR   (or provoke)

FIVE   one another to love and good deeds, not forsaking our own assembling together, as is the habit of some, but encouraging one another."

TWO   James 5:16, "Confess your sins to one another,

ONE   and pray for one another so that you may be healed."

THREE   Accountability is peer pressure, the desire to do right, and a healthy fear of a very real and tangible chastisement, based on God's word, when wrong is done.

FIVE   Accountability means responsibility.

TWO   It means repentance.

FOUR   It means altering our lifestyle to suit God's bidding –

ONE   and not the other way around.

THREE   So, just to be practical, this is a lesson on how to *avoid* accountability.

TWO   One: Isolate yourself.

FOUR   Literally.

FIVE   Don't get close to anyone who might keep you accountable. Even intimidate anyone who tries.

ONE   Two: Isolate yourself with facades. Play the game of Christianity effectively without showing vulnerability or what's really happening inside of you.

TWO   Use all the right words and phrases to keep people thinking you're righteous.

THREE   Three: Neutralize those who would keep you accountable.

ALL   There are plenty of neat ways to do this. You could:

FOUR   Make up reasons why they have no right to keep you accountable.

FIVE   After all, they have sin in their lives too (and be sure to think of some specific examples to throw back at them).

THREE   Accuse them of "judging" you.

ONE   In your mind, dismiss them as self-righteous. Tell them to take the logs out of their own eyes before they try to take the splinter from yours

TWO   (that's always a good one).

FIVE   Debate their theology – make everything a questionable grey area.

FOUR   Believe beyond a shadow of a doubt that they simply don't understand your situation.

THREE   Admit you may have been wrong just to get them to go away – but don't change your behaviour, whatever you do.

TWO   And best of all –

ALL   rationalize.

TWO   Any excuse is a good excuse if you can articulate it well enough.

ONE   The ends justify the means, or,

FIVE   "Since my ministry touches people's lives, my personal lifestyle must be acceptable to God."

THREE   Or, blame someone or something else.

FOUR   Delegate the responsibility, if you know what I mean.

ONE, TWO, THREE & FIVE
        We do.

FOUR   Of course, we all know what becomes of Christians who aren't accountable to anyone –

ALL   but we won't mention names.

TWO   And we certainly don't want you to start thinking
        about it,

ALL   Or you won't learn our lesson!

[They exit. Blackout. Leader takes over.]

QUESTIONS

1. What is accountability? Why is it important?

2. How can you encourage accountability in your life – and
   the lives of the people around you – in very specific areas?
   Think of a person to whom you are, or could be,
   accountable about areas of your life. How do you keep each
   other accountable?

3. In what way/s do you try to avoid or neutralize
   accountability in your life?

Adapted from A Work In Progress *by Paul McCusker.*

2. Family boycott

THEME
Activism.

SITUATION
A husband and wife come face-to-face with the realities of their activism.

CHARACTERS
Rick – a husband.
Jo – a wife.
Kevin – their son (or could be Carla, their daughter).

PLACE
Rick's and Jo's home.

SKIT

[Jo enters with a single grocery bag. Sits down wearily. Rick, her husband, enters.]

RICK   Hi, honey. Where've you been?

JO   The weekly grocery shopping.

RICK   *[Spotting the single bag]* Let me get the rest of the bags in the car. *[Moves to do it]*

JO   No. This is it.

RICK   Our *weekly* groceries? In one bag?

JO   Yes. And I'm exhausted.

[Their son Kevin enters.]

KEVIN   See you later.

RICK   Where are you going?

KEVIN   The movies with a couple of the guys.

RICK   Have fun.

JO   Hold on. Wait a minute. *[She reaches into the grocery bag and produces a clipboard]* What movie?

KEVIN   That new one with Ben Farrell.

JO   *[Finding it on her list]* Lord Of The Matrix?

KEVIN   Yeah.

JO   You can't go. It's a Twentieth-Century Parauniversal production.

KEVIN   So?

JO   So – they're the ones who produced that film about the adulterous evangelist earlier this year, remember? It made Christians look very foolish.

KEVIN   The film or the Christians' reaction to it?

JO   We're boycotting the studio. Pick another film. *[Hands him the clipboard]* From this.

KEVIN   *[Peruses it] Chariots Of Fire* – that's it?

JO   I guess so.

KEVIN   Maybe we'll go to the mall. I need a new pair of trainers.

JO   Fine. Just don't buy any Nick-Bocks. They donate regularly to pro-humanist organizations.

KEVIN   Uh huh.

[Kevin exits.]

RICK   Honey… what was that all about?

JO   You know. You read the newsletter.

RICK   I did. But I don't remember agreeing to do everything it asked us to.

JO   How else are we going to make a point? The companies only listen when we hit them below the money belt. *[Slumping]* I just hope I live to see the victory.

RICK   You're this exhausted over one bag of groceries?

JO   First, I had to find a grocery store that wasn't on the list. Finally found one across town. Then I picked out a cartful of stuff! All the food I like to buy. No sweat. But

then I started checking everything against the list. I got
most of my purchases wrong and had to put them
back. Then, halfway through that, I realized I had last
week's list.

RICK   So? What's a week?

JO   What's a week? Everything! The soap company we were
boycotting last week for testing their products on
animals has reversed their decision, which means that
we're buying their products *this* week to show our
support for their decision. But suddenly I couldn't
remember which soap company! And then I picked up
a spaghetti sauce by a company I could've sworn was
on this week's boycott list for supporting genetically
modified foods in South America – but heard on the
news that it was an unfounded rumour. The spaghetti
sauce company was really tearing up the rain forest for
cattle grazing to get their meat stock, not supporting
genetically modified foods. And suddenly I couldn't
remember which thing we're for and which we're
against. But the company that makes the pasta are
deeply involved with distributing condoms to pre-
adolescents so as of right now you're having spaghetti
sauce on kitty litter. They were the only two things I
could buy.

RICK   This is maddening.

JO   You're telling me? I had a nervous breakdown on the
cereal aisle. I cried, Rick. Openly. The manager came
down to check on me and everything.

RICK   You're kidding. Why?

JO   *[Getting worked up just talking about it]* Because the
newsletter told us to buy General K cereals and avoid
Post Mills for sponsoring that Gay Pride Day – but the
General K cereals had the little Satanic cartoon
character on the front that we're boycotting and… and
I couldn't decide whether I was supposed to buy the

cereal or not! It was the worst moral dilemma I've ever faced! *[She weeps loudly]*

RICK   There, there... it's all right. You're doing your best.

JO   It's all so complicated.

RICK   I know, I know. Look, forget about shopping. Let's go out – just the two of us – and get something to eat.

JO   *[Sniffling]* That would be nice. *[Thrusts the clipboard into his hand]* Pick somewhere.

[Freeze. Blackout. (Cast exits.) The discussion leader takes over.]

QUESTIONS

1. We live in an age of political activism, for all sorts of causes, and demands are made on us constantly to show companies where we stand through the purchases we make (or don't make). What do you think of this philosophy? Do you think companies are persuaded to change their policies because of boycotts?

2. Have you ever actively avoided buying products from a company because of their policies related to a particular cause? If yes, what company and why did you take action against them? Do you know if it had any effect?

3. Academics

THEME
Application of Christian knowledge.

SITUATION
In which a diligent student of the Bible has trouble finding time to actually do what he's learning about.

CHARACTERS
Al – a study-weary Christian.
Don – a concerned friend.

PLACE
A church hallway.

▬▬▬

SKIT

[Al is walking across the stage. Don follows, trying to catch up.]

DON   Hey, Al!

AL   *[Startled]* What?

DON   Relax. Why so jumpy?

AL   You're going to ask me to do something, aren't you? I can't go anywhere around this church without somebody asking me to do something.

DON   Well, I –

AL   I can't do it so don't ask.

DON   Do what?

AL   Whatever you're going to ask me to do.

DON   I was only wondering how you're doing. I haven't seen you in a while – not since you started that university course on theology. How's it going? Are you learning a lot?

AL   Are you kidding? Who has time to learn? I'm too busy! I have a philosophy paper due tomorrow that you wouldn't believe. I have to prove the existence of God and refute any possible arguments – in 200 words or less.

DON   That's incredible.

AL   And I'm taking a class in world religions that has me running ragged. You can't imagine the assignments. I have to interview a Buddhist, a Muslim, a Hare Krishna and a Mormon, with a complete written explanation of their beliefs. By Tuesday.

DON   Wow.

AL   Do you know how long it took me just to find them?

DON   Quite a while I would imagine, but –

AL   Tonight I have a meeting of the Eschatology Club. I
      don't even know what Eschatology is! And I'm President!
      All we ever do is sit around looking at calendars.

DON   Sounds like you are busy.

AL   And after that I have to go home and read the entire Old
      Testament – putting in chronological order chapter and
      verse for my Bible class.

DON   That's tough. When do you sleep?

AL   The only time I have left. In class.

DON   Amazing. But I'm sure you're getting a lot out of it, huh?

AL   *[Pause]* Like what?

DON   You're studying theology, right? Surely all that time in
      the Bible is giving you ideas.

AL   Ideas?

DON   How to be a better Christian. You know, put it all into
      practical application.

AL   Well... ah... Practical Applications is an upper-level course.

DON   And prayer. Your prayer-life must be top quality, I'll bet.

AL   Prayer? Ah... that's not until next semester.

DON   Then it must be stimulating being with those other
      students – people studying the Bible together – almost
      like a church, huh?

AL   I'm at the library all the time. No talking.

DON   Developing discipline? Commitment?

AL   *[Shakes head]* Electives. I don't have time to take those. I would, though.

DON   Wait a minute. You're telling me you don't use what you study, you don't pray, you don't meet with other Christians... why are you studying theology?

AL   So I can become a Pastor! *[He begins backing away, hurried again]* Just wait. In four years I'll be perfect. *[Turns, exits]*

DON   *[Shrugs, moves to exit]* Somehow I doubt it. *[Exits]*

[Blackout. The discussion leader takes over.]

QUESTIONS

1. Reference Ecclesiastes 12:9–14 and James 1:22. How do you think they're relevant to this scene?

2. What are your feelings about Al's "predicament" – being so overwhelmed with studies? Do you know anyone like Al? Can you empathize with Al at all? If you can, in what way/s?

3. What can you do about having such a hectic schedule? What advice would you give to someone like Al about his life, if any?

4. Do you find it difficult to maintain a balance between your study of the Bible and putting what you learn into practice? If you do, how can you work to find balance? If not, how do you consciously find such a balanced life, if any?

4. Clichés

THEME
Articulating inner faith.

SITUATION
A monologue, in which our character sets us straight about doubt and confusion.

CHARACTERS
Karen (or could be a male)

PLACE
Anywhere.

NOTE
There are two versions of this sketch, one is written for a British audience, the other is written for an American audience.

SKIT (VERSION ONE – UK)

[Our character enters.]

KAREN I have a few things to say about faith and doubt. You
see, I've found in my walk with the Lord that my quiet
times help defeat any struggle with confusion I might
have as a believer. Remember: Satan is the author of
confusion, but God owns the bookshop. And if God
says it and I believe it, then that's good enough for me.
Tonight I was given a word of knowledge. That word
was *renewal*. We need to ally our evangelicals, care for
the family, and spring to the harvest. We're all the
King's kids who must remember that Christianity isn't
a religion, it's a way of life. Simply let go and let God,
for He hates sin, but loves the sinner. He's for us. Trust
and obey. We must tell the nations about the King's
way by giving shouts of joy on our march for Jesus.
With meekness and majesty, we have to let shine Jesus
shine while we live under the shadow of His wing in
this present darkness. Oh, Lord, glorify Thy name.

[Exits. Blackout. The discussion leader takes over.]

SKIT (VERSION TWO – US)

[Our character enters.]

KAREN   Hi, I'm Karen. Y'know, I've found in my walk with the Lord that my quiet times help defeat any struggle with doubt I might have as a believer. Remember: Satan may be the author of confusion, but God owns the bookstore. And if God says it and I believe it, then that's good enough for me. We need to get back to the Bible, focus on the family, and pray to have insight for living. We can't afford to be addicted to mediocrity because Christianity isn't a religion, it's a way of life. Just let go and let God, for He hates sin, but loves the sinner. He's the real thing. Trust and obey. Give the Master charge by putting your hand in the hand of the One who stilled the water. O, Lord, glorify Your name.

[Exits. Blackout. The discussion leader takes over.]

QUESTIONS

1. How do you react to someone who speaks as this character speaks? Are you assured of their faith and take encouragement about your own faith? Do you know anyone who believes – or talks – as this character talks? What do you think of such a person? Do you agree with them or disagree? Explain.

2. Some believe that doubt is an important ingredient to a life of faith (author Frederick Buechner called doubt the "ants in the pants of faith"). Do you agree or disagree? Explain your point of view.

3. Some believe that doubt is a faith destroyer. Do you agree or disagree? Please explain.

Adapted from A Work In Progress *and* You Say Tomato: The Transatlantic Correspondence of George & Brad *by Adrian Plass and Paul McCusker.*

5. Exegetical explanations

THEME
Articulating the faith.

SITUATION
A young man (or woman) attempts to articulate the essence of faith.

CHARACTERS
Gareth (or Ruth)

PLACE
Anywhere.

SKIT

[Gareth enters.]

GARETH   Hello, I'm Gareth. I think we live in a time when many people are searching for transcendent experiences, wondering about their places in the Universe, about God, about the relevancy of Christian teaching. I certainly understand those questions. But I've found that once the Gospel – the Good News, the heavenly proclamation – was explained to them in a clear, exegetical manner – once they grasped the redemptive nature of the cross, providing propitiation for our sins and reconciling us to Him as both justified and sanctified – a holy people, set apart for His greater purposes which He foreknew before the beginning of time itself – that there was nothing left to be confused about. At least, it's crystal clear to me.

[Exits. Blackout. The discussion leader takes over.]

QUESTIONS

1. What did he say? Try to translate this monologue into your own words.

2. Even if some Christians understood him, do you think any of those outside the Christian faith would?

Adapted from A Work In Progress *by Paul McCusker.*

6. Len's birthday

THEME
Befriending the unpopular.

SITUATION
In which an unpopular kid at school has a birthday and gets a card.

CHARACTERS
Jason – regular guy, popular athlete at school.
Len – the school "outcast". He should be dressed unfashionably, with thick glasses (taped at the bridge), and a pocket full of pens (with ink stain at the bottom of the pocket). His school uniform should be immaculate, though.
Brad – another student, passing by.

PLACE
A bench at a school.

SKIT

*[A bench outside a school. Jason enters with his books, sits down
and opens one, looking through it without much concentration.
Swiftly, Len appears carrying books, spots Jason and approaches him
before Jason can do anything about it.]*

LEN   Hi, Jason!

JASON   *[Winces]* Hi, Len.

LEN   *[Sitting down next to him]* Whatcha doing?

JASON   Reading.

LEN   No kidding. I thought you were playing ping pong.
           [Laughs loudly, elbows Jason who doesn't react] Whatcha
           reading?

JASON   Biology.

LEN   Isn't Biology neat? It's my favourite class. All those cells
           and chromosomes and stuff.

JASON   I hate it.

LEN   Yeah, well, I don't like it that much either.

JASON   I think it's stupid.

LEN   Yeah, real naff.

JASON   *[Slamming book closed, frustrated]* It's a waste of time.

LEN   Yeah. *[Pause/Beat]* I could help you with it, Jason. I
           mean, I don't like it but I'm pretty good at it. Do you
           want me to help you, Jason? Maybe we could meet at
           your house one afternoon.

JASON   Yeah, yeah, maybe.

LEN   How about this afternoon? You wanna study together this afternoon?

JASON   Not this afternoon, Len. I'm busy.

LEN   Football practice, huh? I'll bet you have football practice.

JASON   No, I –

LEN   Then let's get together today. Okay? You can come over today.

JASON   I can't. I have... *[Tries to think of something]* Other things to do.

LEN   Yeah, so do I. Today's my birthday and I'm having a party this afternoon. You wanna come to my birthday party, Jason? It'll be a blast!

JASON   I don't think so. Like I said, I'm pretty busy this afternoon.

LEN   If I change it to tonight, will you come? I'll change it to tonight. It's only me and my mum anyway. Will you come tonight?

JASON   I'm busy tonight, too.

LEN   Boy, you're a real busy guy, aren't you? Betcha have a date tonight, don't you?

JASON   *[Grabbing onto this thought as an excuse]* Yeah! That's it. I have a date. I'm going out with... Alice. Yeah, I'm going out with Alice.

LEN   But you can't be! I asked Alice to my birthday party and she said she couldn't because she was going out with Frank.

JASON   *What?*

LEN   So you can come tonight. Oh, good!

JASON   Whoa, now. I meant another Alice. You don't know
        her.

LEN   You can bring her with you, Jason. You can bring your
        date. We'll have soda pop and party hats and cake and
        we'll play Pin-The-Tail-On-The-Donkey and Blind-
        Man's-Bluff and –

JASON   No, Len, I can't.

LEN   Okay, Jason, maybe you can come to my birthday party
        next year. Will you come next year?

JASON   I'll probably be busy next year, too.

LEN   Wow. Got a date next year, too?

JASON   I hope so. Look, Len, I gotta go. *[Moves to leave]*

LEN   Hey, Jason, wait... *[Fishes through papers, produces
        birthday card]* I have this birthday card...

JASON   Good for you.

LEN   I mean, I bought it myself.

JASON   You bought your own birthday card?

LEN   Yeah... I was wondering if you would sign it.

JASON   Huh?

LEN   You don't even have to say anything special. Just sign
        it... will you? Please?

JASON   *[Very uncomfortable with this]* I... I don't think so.

LEN   All you have to put is your name. You don't even have
          to write "Happy Birthday" or "Love" or anything
          mushy.

JASON   *[Hesitates, then takes it and reads the card – he laughs]*
          This is a pretty funny card.

LEN   *[Laughs, excited]* Yeah. I picked it out myself.

JASON   *[Signs card]* There. *[Hands it back to Len. Len looks at it
          with delight]* And… happy birthday, Len.

LEN   Thanks, Jason! Wow!

JASON   Sure. *[Gathers things]* I gotta go. *[He exits. Len looks at his
          birthday card proudly. Brad walks past.]*

LEN   Hey, Brad!

BRAD   *[Winces]* Yeah, Len?

LEN   *[Gathering his things, stands, shows Brad the birthday card]*
          Look at what Jason did for my birthday. See? He signed
          it himself!

[They begin to walk away.]

BRAD   Jason?

LEN   Yeah! *[Points to signature]* See?

BRAD   *[Impressed]* Hmmmm… Happy birthday, Len.

LEN   Thanks! You wanna come to a party tonight, Brad? I'm
          gonna have a birthday party.

BRAD   Well… I don't know. Alice and I are supposed to go out.

[Exit. Blackout. The discussion leader takes over.]

QUESTIONS

1. Do you know people like Len? How do you feel when you
   are around them? How do you treat them when you are
   alone with them? How do you treat them when you are
   with your friends?

2. How are you like Len? What needs and wants does he have
   that you have as well?

3. People like Len are often ignored, laughed at or picked on.
   Is that true in your school or church? If it is, why do you
   think that happens? Should it happen? What does the Bible
   say about our behaviour towards one another? How would
   you apply such principles to relationships with the
   "outcasts" in our lives?

4. Reference John 15:12; Ephesians 5:2; Matthew 5:43–48; I
   John 3:13–18. How do these verses apply to this sketch?

7. **Nice**

THEME
Being Christ-like.

SITUATION
An encounter in which a church leader asks a member not to return to church.

CHARACTERS
Church leader
Offender

Note: either of these characters could be male or female.

PLACE
The home of the offender.

SKIT

[A couple of chairs can represent the living room. The two characters enter, as if the offender has just asked the church leader to come in.]

CHURCH LEADER   Thanks for seeing me.

OFFENDER   No problem. What's going on? Why the long face?

CHURCH LEADER   I'm afraid I have some bad news.

OFFENDER   Oh? What's wrong?

CHURCH LEADER   I... well, the leadership at the church asked me to speak with you.

OFFENDER   About what?

CHURCH LEADER   This is very difficult. You see, they – well, *we* – don't want you to come back to our fellowship.

OFFENDER   What? You're throwing me out of the church?

CHURCH LEADER   That's not how I'd put it, but... well, yes. We are.

OFFENDER   Why? What have I done wrong?

CHURCH LEADER   As you know, our church was founded on the belief that we as Christians are to be Christ-like.

OFFENDER   Yes, yes, I know that. I agree with it.

CHURCH LEADER   Maybe you *think* you do, but your behaviour demonstrates otherwise.

OFFENDER   What do you mean? Please, I want to know.
                  Give me some examples.

CHURCH LEADER   The main thing, I suppose, is that you aren't
                  very... uh... nice.

OFFENDER   Nice?

CHURCH LEADER   That's right. You are, at times, very...
                  confrontational... direct, if you know what I
                  mean. It makes people uncomfortable. Like
                  with Rose the other night. You told her to
                  her face that she was gossiping and shouldn't
                  be doing it.

OFFENDER   Yes. I wasn't mean or unkind to her, but I
                  thought she should know that –

CHURCH LEADER   But you said it to her *face*.

OFFENDER   Yes, I know. But we were alone. I didn't make
                  a scene in front of anyone else. In fact, I
                  didn't want anyone else to know. But I
                  believed she should be told that –

CHURCH LEADER   The point I'm trying to make is that it wasn't
                  a nice thing to do. And if we're to be like
                  Jesus, then we need to be... well, *nice* to
                  people.

OFFENDER   Really?

CHURCH LEADER   Yes. And you're not very nice. You called Fred
                  a hypocrite.

OFFENDER   But only because he is.

CHURCH LEADER   I know he is. *Everyone* knows he is. But it
                  wasn't very nice for you to say it.

OFFENDER   Privately. To his face.

CHURCH LEADER   At *all*.

OFFENDER   Hmm.

CHURCH LEADER   And then there's this whole mess you've created with our Evangelism class.

OFFENDER   What mess?

CHURCH LEADER   Well, you know that we're trying to bring people into the church – we want them to become Christians. We think that's very important.

OFFENDER   So do I.

CHURCH LEADER   Yes, but you... you're putting them off.

OFFENDER   How?

CHURCH LEADER   You go on and on about things like the *cost of discipleship* and how we must sacrifice ourselves and be willing to give everything up to follow Him and... I think you know what I'm talking about. It's a turn-off. We want to get them saved and *then* let them in on the responsibilities. But what you're doing is... uh...

OFFENDER   Not nice.

CHURCH LEADER   Right. You want to be like Jesus who invited everyone into His kingdom. You've got to be nice. He certainly was.

OFFENDER   Was He? So when He called the religious leaders "white-washed tombs" or got impatient with the disciples for their lack of faith or told them that, to follow Him, they'd have to hate their own families and pick up their crosses and maybe even die... He was being *nice*?

CHURCH LEADER   When you put it like *that*... no.

OFFENDER   I wouldn't know how else to put it.

CHURCH LEADER   Which is exactly the problem! And that's why I have to ask you to... well, find another fellowship. Maybe there's another church out there that'll meet your needs. One that isn't so...

OFFENDER   Nice.

CHURCH LEADER   Right. Thanks for your understanding. Goodnight. *[He/she goes]*

OFFENDER   *[Shrugs]* I guess I've been following the wrong Jesus. *[Exits]*

[Blackout. The discussion leader takes over.]

QUESTIONS

1. How would you define *nice*? Was Jesus nice? Why or why not?

2. When we talk about "being Christ-like" what do we mean? If you were to try to behave like Christ, what would you do? How, exactly, does one become "Christ-like"?

3. Though it may not seem "nice", are there times when we should confront other Christians about their questionable behaviour? When and under what circumstance/s? By what authority, if any, do we have the right to confront others?

8. Men of God

THEME
Being men of God.

SITUATION
Two men discuss Godliness in their lives after a men's retreat.

CHARACTERS
Jim
Bob

PLACE
Anywhere.

▬▬▬

SKIT

[Jim and Bob approach each other.]

JIM   Bob, Bob, Bob...

BOB   Hiya, Jim.

[They hug, giving each other bruising pats on the back as they do. Afterwards, as they continue to talk, they subconsciously adjust their shoulders to accommodate the pain.]

JIM   Thanks for meeting me. I really appreciate it.

BOB   Hey, that's what I'm here for, right? What's going on?

JIM   It's my life, Bob. My life. Ever since the men's getaway we did at the church.

BOB   Ever since? It was only two days ago.

JIM   Two very long days.

BOB   You better tell me about it.

JIM   I will. Y'know, I got home and it was like... like Moses coming down from the mountaintop, carrying with him all those animals. Two by two. Just glowing from being up there with –

BOB   You mean ten commandments, don't you?

JIM   Huh?

BOB   Moses carried the ten commandments. It was Noah who had the animals. He put them in the Ark.

JIM   I thought that was David.

BOB   David who?

JIM   King David.

BOB   King David didn't have any animals.

JIM   But he had an Ark. Remember? God struck a bunch of his
      men dead for opening it.

BOB   No. God struck one of David's *guards* for *touching* it.

JIM   I distinctly remember God striking some men dead for
      opening it. It's as clear as if I saw it myself.

BOB   You did see it, Jim. In *Raiders Of The Lost Ark*. Indiana
      Jones, remember? God zapped the Nazis at the end for
      opening the Ark of the Covenant.

JIM   That makes sense.

BOB   It does?

JIM   Sure! God didn't want them to let all the animals out.

BOB   Jim –

JIM   But, you see, that gets right at the heart of the problem.
      You just said it.

BOB   You've got problems with animals?

JIM   No. Indiana Jones.

BOB   You better explain.

JIM   I will. Ever since I got home from our men's retreat, it's
      like my family expects me to be Indiana Jones. Y'know –
      a man's man around the house.

BOB   How so?

JIM   My wife. I get home and she's looking at me with that
      expression of hers. You know it?

BOB   Not really.

JIM   Rosy cheeks, big eyes.

BOB   What does that mean?

JIM   It means that she expects me to remember to take out the trash and mow the lawn and remodel the spare room... y'know, all the things I promised to do.

BOB   Oh, I get it.

JIM   And in the bedroom... my word!

BOB   What?

JIM   It's awful. I'd have to be an Olympic gymnast to do all the things she wants me to do.

BOB   Uh, Jim –

JIM   She's got me running all over the place.

BOB   I really don't think I want to hear this –

JIM   I mean, I never knew making the bed could be so difficult. I have to tuck in the corner over here then run over to the other side to tuck in that corner and... well, those king-sized beds are a killer. And she's very particular.

BOB   *[Relieved]* I see. Okay. Good.

JIM   What's wrong? What did you think I was talking about?

BOB   Nothing. Never mind.

JIM   And my son keeps telling all the other kids at school that I can beat up their fathers.

BOB   Kids are like that when they're young.

JIM   Yeah, but my son's in college!

BOB   Oh.

JIM   I felt like a real idiot fighting with Mr Henderson.
      Especially when he got me in that headlock and gave me
      noogies. It was embarrassing!

BOB   I'll bet.

JIM   You can be sure that Indiana Jones never got noogies.

BOB   Probably not.

JIM   It just doesn't make sense – that's what I'm trying to say.
      I'm really confused. What was that men's retreat all
      about?

BOB   It was about *this*.

JIM   What *this*?

BOB   What we're doing right now. You and me – talking about
      it. Look, if I learned nothing else from our time together,
      it's that we need each other. There's nothing wrong or
      weak or flawed about men needing men. To talk. To
      support. To help.

JIM   Yeah but… I feel like such a wisp.

BOB   You mean *wimp*.

JIM   You think so, too.

BOB   Not at all. There's nothing wimpy about needing help.

JIM   *[Beat]* Can I ask one more question?

BOB   Go ahead.

JIM   Why do men always beat each other half-to-death when they hug?

BOB   I dunno. I guess to show that we're not enjoying it too much. Come on, let's go down to Starbrick's and I'll get the first round of coffee.

JIM   How many rounds do you think we'll have?

BOB   Depends on how much help you need.

JIM   Could be a lot, then.

[Exit. Blackout. The discussion leader takes over.]

QUESTIONS

1. What does it mean to be a "man of God"? How would you describe or characterize such a man?

2. In what way/s can men – and women – encourage each other in their faith?

3. What does the Bible say about "communities" of faith? What characteristics do they share? Do you think the modern church shares those characteristics? How does it – or doesn't it?

9. Too nice

THEME
Break-up of a marriage.

SITUATION
A woman comes home, just as her husband is leaving her.

CHARACTERS
Karen
Jim, Karen's husband

PLACE
The front hall at Karen's and Jim's.

━━━
SKIT

[Karen enters, carrying her Bible and notebook from an evening Bible study. She is happy and chatty.]

KAREN   *[Putting her things down]* Honey! I'm home! Sorry I'm late but we started talking about lots of interesting things in our Bible class. "Being in the world, but not of it..." "The sovereignty of God..." things like that. We didn't even get beyond the first verse of our text tonight. *[Pause/Beat]* Jim? Jim! I found this lovely poster at the Fishnet Bookstore. It says "Be Patient. God isn't finished with me yet." Isn't that a cute saying? Jim? *[Puts poster on table/sideboard]*

[Jim enters, carrying a suitcase.]

KAREN   Oh, there you are. What's this?

JIM   I'm sorry. There's a note for you on the bed. I thought I'd be gone before you got home.

KAREN   Gone? But I don't understand.

JIM   Sure you do.

KAREN   But... we're supposed to start counselling. You said –

JIM   It's too late for counselling. It's all in the note.

KAREN   Too late? It's never too late, Jim.

JIM   It is for me. Karen, please, you knew this was coming. I thought we were going to keep it simple.

KAREN   Simple! You're leaving me, aren't you? You thought that would be simple? *[With resolve]* We can make it work, Jim. All we have to do is try a little harder. We'll make more time for each other.

JIM   I don't want more time.

KAREN   Then what *do* you want? Are you tired of being married
         – the responsibilities?

JIM   No.

KAREN   You just want some time to yourself.

JIM   No.

KAREN   Then what is it?

JIM   Just read the note.

KAREN   I don't want to read the note. Tell me.

JIM   I don't love you anymore. The love isn't there. I feel
         like – I don't feel anything.

KAREN   *[Shocked]* Nothing at all?

JIM   *[Shakes his head no]* I don't. You're a very sweet girl.
         So... nice. Too nice, maybe. It's in the note, Karen. I
         have to go. *[He moves to exit]*

KAREN   You know this is wrong. What you're doing is *very*
         wrong. Love is a commitment. It's an act of the will.
         You can choose.

JIM   I know the clichés, Karen, but I'm not going to think
         about them now.

KAREN   But... there are things we have to sort out.

JIM   Our lawyers can work them out.

KAREN   *[Surprised]* You have a lawyer?

JIM   Yes. *[Pause/Beat]* Goodbye, Karen.

[Jim exits. She stands numbly.]

KAREN Goodbye, Jim.

[She slumps down in her chair. Her eye catches the poster – she tears it in two and puts her face in her hands.]

[Blackout. Karen exits. The discussion leader takes over.]

QUESTIONS

1. What is your impression of Karen's personality. Do you know anyone like her? From the scene, what has happened to this marriage?

2. Do you agree with Jim's action? Why or why not? Under what circumstances do you think separation and/or divorce is understandable or acceptable? Is Jim's reason – that he feels nothing for Karen – a legitimate reason to leave her?

3. Jim referenced Karen's "clichés" – what do you think he meant by that? Jim also suggested that Karen was "too nice". What do you think he meant?

4. One might get the impression – from the clues about Karen's activities, the things she mentions as soon as she gets home, the poster she bought at the Christian bookstore – that Karen seems to have her faith figured out. Yet, at the end, she tears the poster up. What do you think that signifies?

Adapted from A Work In Progress *by Paul McCusker.*

10. In the ghetto

THEME
Christian consumerism.

SITUATION
Two women discuss the various Christian products that enrich their lives.

CHARACTERS
Sarah
Becky
Frank

PLACE
Around a kitchen table.

▬▬

SKIT

[Sarah and Becky enter with their cups (or mugs) of tea and sit down at the table.]

BECKY   *[Putting her cup down]* That was a wonderful cup of tea. Bless You?

SARAH   Yes, it is.

BECKY   It was very shrewd of the Tetley's company to start a Christian line of tea. Bless You Tea... Heavenly Irish Breakfast...

SARAH   Praise Pekoe is my favourite.

BECKY   Perfect for a beautiful afternoon of fellowship. And that music... *[She listens]* What are we listening to?

SARAH   *The Praise Him In All His Glory Collection*... Volume 173.

BECKY   I just bought the children's version for my kids.

SARAH   I was reading in *Contemporary Christian Lifestyle* magazine that they're releasing it as an animated video. With that cute little character – the one with the effeminate voice – looks like a kitchen utensil.

BECKY   Oh – Saltshaker! I'll have to go down to the Sonshine Bookshop and put in an order. My kids love him. *[Singing]* "Shake a little here... shake a little there... the Salt of the Earth should be everywhere!" It's so comforting to know that somebody's doing something to keep my children from being contaminated by worldly videos.

SARAH   I saw a report on the *Trinity Praise News Hour* that said our children are more susceptible to worldly influence through the media now than any other time in history.

They're being brainwashed by humanistic philosophies masquerading as cartoon character heroes!

BECKY   Don't I know it. That's why I've put all three of my children in the David And Goliath Day Care and Whole Armour Of God Christian School. I won't have them exposed to that sort of thing. Little Isaiah wants to be a missionary, you know.

SARAH   You said.

BECKY   He came up with the idea all by himself. No pressure from me and Joe at all. We want to be sensitive to our children's inner spirits. Have you read Dr Jameson's latest?

SARAH   No.

BECKY   *What Strong-willed Children Wish Their Parents Knew About Discipline In Love.* It's fabulous.

SARAH   Maybe when I have children.

BECKY   Oh, Sarah. I'm sorry. I didn't mean to –

SARAH   That's all right, Becky. We've handed it over to Him. In His good time we'll be fruitful and multiply.

BECKY   I know you will. It isn't God's will that you should be deprived of the joy.

SARAH   I know. But He's working it out for the good. I'm starting my own ministry.

BECKY   Really?

SARAH   Yes. I've been praying about it for quite a while and I can see now why God hasn't given us children. He wants me to have more time for Him, for what He's called me to do.

BECKY   I'm ready to burst. What is it?

SARAH   Refrigerator magnets.

BECKY   No.

SARAH   Yes. I'm going to use my talents to create refrigerator
         magnets that have little Bible verses on them – with
         cute little animals and characters, too.

BECKY   I'm getting goose bumps. Think of the lives you'll
         touch!

SARAH   Not me.

BECKY   Of course. The Lord.

SARAH   The Logos Network, actually.

BECKY   I beg your pardon?

SARAH   The Logos Network. They're a Christian distributing
         company. They market to Christian bookstores all over
         the country.

BECKY   How exciting! *[Pause/Beat, looks at her watch, rises]* Oh,
         Sarah, I'm sorry. I have to go. My car is at the
         Mechanics Of The Master Garage and they asked me to
         pick it up by two.

SARAH   Are they a good service centre?

BECKY   Absolutely! I wouldn't take my car anywhere else!

SARAH   I've taken my car over to the Lube Job For The Lord
         Garage but, well, Frank doesn't have a lot of faith in
         their work. *[Near whisper]* In fact, he doesn't even like
         to take our car to a Christian garage. He says "either the
         mechanics are good and honest or they're not – what
         does being Christian have to do with it?" I worry about

him sometimes. I think he's under attack by some very questionable influences at work.

BECKY   Well, the men at Mechanics Of The Master actually pray over their cars. They've even had their tools anointed! It makes all the difference, I'm sure.

[Frank enters, excitedly.]

FRANK   I can't believe it, I can't believe it! Quick – turn on the TV!

SARAH   Frank? What's wrong?

FRANK   China has just renounced communism and ousted their government. They're going to form a democracy!

[Frank exits the other side.]

SARAH   *[Calling after him]* Don't you touch that TV! I have the VCR set for the *Thrilled By The Spirit Miracle Message Show*!

FRANK   *[From off-stage]* Who cares?

BECKY   I see what you mean. I'll add him to my prayer list.

SARAH   Thanks.

BECKY   Gotta run.

SARAH   I'll walk you to the door.

[Exit. Blackout. The discussion leader takes over.]

QUESTIONS

1. What do you think of Sarah and Becky? Do you know anyone like them?

2. What do you think was the point of this sketch?

3. How easy is it to become completely absorbed in and surrounded by "Christianity"? In what way/s might that be healthy? In what way/s might it be unhealthy?

4. Frank, Sarah's husband, is quoted as saying: "either the mechanics are good and honest or they're not – what does being Christian have to do with it?" Do you agree or disagree with him (not only about mechanics specifically, but other workers in other vocations)?

5. Is it good to have "Christian alternatives" to books, music, movies, television shows or even other types of products? Why or why not?

Adapted from A Work In Progress *by Paul McCusker.*

11. **Unity**

THEME
Church unity.

SITUATION
Two character discuss church unity.

CHARACTERS
Character One
Character Two

Note: either could be male or female.

PLACE
Outside a church.

SKIT

[Our two characters enter.]

ONE   I'm worried about our church.

TWO   Why? What's wrong?

ONE   We're not... well, of one mind. Unified.

TWO   I don't agree with that.

ONE   I wouldn't expect you to.

TWO   Why not?

ONE   Because we're not unified. That's my point. You don't agree with anything I say.

TWO   That's not true.

ONE   Yes it is.

TWO   No it isn't.

ONE   Of course it is. You're disagreeing with me now.

TWO   But that's because you're wrong.

ONE   In your opinion.

TWO   Not just *my* opinion.

ONE   Oh, there are others who think I'm wrong?

TWO   Yes.

ONE   Well I happen to know that there are some who think I'm right.

TWO The wrong ones.

ONE Or the right ones.

TWO So you say.

ONE So I do. Which proves exactly what I'm saying.

TWO What are you saying?

ONE That we're not unified.

TWO We can disagree and still be unified.

ONE No we can't.

TWO Yes we can. We're doing it now.

ONE How?

TWO By standing here arguing about whether or not we're unified. I'm still here. You're still here. And when the music starts we'll go in for the service.

ONE No we won't.

TWO Yes we will.

ONE No we won't. I'm on my way home from the nine o'clock service. You go to the ten o'clock service.

TWO You're right. And I'm going to be late. *[Rushes off]*

ONE You see? We're not unified.

[Exits. Blackout. The discussion leader takes over.]

QUESTIONS

1. What does it mean for a church to be "of one mind"?
   Describe the characteristics of a church that is "of one
   mind".

2. Explain how a church can and should be united. In what
   way/s can there be disagreements within the church, and
   yet it can remain united?

3. Describe the many ways in which a church can be torn
   apart. What are the effects on the people within the
   church? How might divisions affect people outside of the
   church?

4. What practical things can a church do to strengthen its
   unity and ward off divisions?

12. **A case of communication**

THEME
Communication.

SITUATION
A London detective interviews an American tourist about a crime.

CHARACTERS
Detective
American tourist

PLACE
The lobby of a hotel.

Note
This sketch needs to be played very straight, with neither character understanding the other, but persevering anyway.

SKIT

[The detective and visitor drift on stage, talking as they do. The detective is carrying a small pad of paper, into which he writes notes.]

DETECTIVE   Right. So you're our witness.

AMERICAN TOURIST   I think so.

DETECTIVE   Tell me what happened.

AMERICAN TOURIST   Well, I'm here on vacation –

DETECTIVE   Holiday.

AMERICAN TOURIST   I don't know what holiday. I just came over on vacation for a couple of weeks.

DETECTIVE   Fortnight.

AMERICAN TOURIST   No – for a couple of weeks. And I'm staying in a room up on the second floor and I came down to the lobby –

DETECTIVE   Did you take the stairs?

AMERICAN TOURIST   Oh no, I didn't feel like walking the two storeys.

DETECTIVE   Three storeys.

AMERICAN TOURIST   Two. I'm in a room on the *second* floor.

DETECTIVE   Right. That's three up.

AMERICAN TOURIST   No, it's *two*.

DETECTIVE   Never mind. You didn't take the stairs, you used the lifts.

AMERICAN TOURIST   Actually, I was wearing sneakers. I only use lifts on formal occasions to get more height.

DETECTIVE   Really.

AMERICAN TOURIST   Yeah. Anyway, I got on the elevator to come down here to the lobby on the first floor.

DETECTIVE   Ground floor.

AMERICAN TOURIST   Bottom floor.

DETECTIVE   Whatever. The lobby.

AMERICAN TOURIST   Because I wanted to go to a pharmacy –

DETECTIVE   Chemist's –

AMERICAN TOURIST   More than likely. So I asked the receptionist –

DETECTIVE   Desk clerk. [Pronounced "clark"]

AMERICAN TOURIST   I don't know his name. But he recommended a place down the main street.

DETECTIVE   High street.

AMERICAN TOURIST   Might've been uphill, I don't know. As I was walking, I thought I'd stop at a fast-food place and get some fish and some french fries.

DETECTIVE   Chips.

AMERICAN TOURIST   They didn't have any, so I got the french fries. Then it started to rain and I thought I'd step into the store –

DETECTIVE	Shop.
AMERICAN TOURIST	Yes, to do that. I wanted to buy an umbrella –
DETECTIVE	Brolly.
AMERICAN TOURIST	No, thanks. Anyway, it was pouring down so hard that I rushed back here and nearly got hit outside on the pedestrian crossing.
DETECTIVE	Zebra crossing.
AMERICAN TOURIST	No, they were cars.
DETECTIVE	Now, let me get something straight. You legged it back *why*?
AMERICAN TOURIST	Legged? Back? I don't have problems with either. I guess if I did I couldn't have rushed back.
DETECTIVE	But you said –
AMERICAN TOURIST	It was pouring.
DETECTIVE	What was?
AMERICAN TOURIST	The rain.
DETECTIVE	I see. And that's when you saw the suspect. He was, I understand, humping his bags down the hallway.
AMERICAN TOURIST	I didn't see anything like *that*.
DETECTIVE	Then what did you see?
AMERICAN TOURIST	The cleaning lady –
DETECTIVE	Maid.

AMERICAN TOURIST Not sure what she made, but she seemed to be asleep in a chair in the hall. And he knocked her flat out of the chair onto her rump.

DETECTIVE "Knocked her flat out of the chair"?

AMERICAN TOURIST That's right.

DETECTIVE "Onto her rump"?

AMERICAN TOURIST Yes.

DETECTIVE Bum.

AMERICAN TOURIST I thought so, too. Though he was dressed in some pretty nice clothes.

DETECTIVE So he knocked over the maid and she fell to the floor.

AMERICAN TOURIST Yes.

DETECTIVE And then what?

AMERICAN TOURIST I was so angry that I followed him down.

DETECTIVE In the lift?

AMERICAN TOURIST Sneakers.

DETECTIVE Ah. He was trying to be quiet. Got it.

AMERICAN TOURIST And then he went out to the front of the hotel and threw his suitcase into the trunk of the car.

DETECTIVE Into a trunk? Was it sitting next to the car?

AMERICAN TOURIST No, the back.

DETECTIVE	And this went into the boot?
AMERICAN TOURIST	I didn't notice his shoes. Then, as he was pulling away in his car, this truck came along and *bang*.
DETECTIVE	A lorry.
AMERICAN TOURIST	Didn't catch his name.
DETECTIVE	Then what can you tell me about him – the driver, that is.
AMERICAN TOURIST	He was a real idiot.
DETECTIVE	A wally.
AMERICAN TOURIST	I didn't catch his name. But he hit the car, backed up and looked like he'd do it again.
DETECTIVE	He hit the car twice? With what, his fists?
AMERICAN TOURIST	His front end.
DETECTIVE	Ouch. That must've hurt.
AMERICAN TOURIST	He didn't seem hurt. Because he backed up again and drove off.
DETECTIVE	Drove off? In what – the lorry?
AMERICAN TOURIST	No, the truck. Like I said, I didn't catch any names. Wally… Laurie… I don't know. But it was pretty bad. Knocked the muffler right off.
DETECTIVE	Off who?
AMERICAN TOURIST	The car.
DETECTIVE	There was a *muffler* on the car?

AMERICAN TOURIST	Sure. Is that so strange?
DETECTIVE	I've never seen anyone wrap their car in a muffler. Not in warm weather anyway.
AMERICAN TOURIST	The *muffler* – the thing that's on the bottom, near the back.
DETECTIVE	Wait. I think you mean a *silencer*.
AMERICAN TOURIST	No guns were involved that I could see.
DETECTIVE	*[Groans]* So what happened next?
AMERICAN TOURIST	That was it. The truck went one way up to the traffic lights –
DETECTIVE	The T-junction.
AMERICAN TOURIST	The car went the other way to the circle.
DETECTIVE	Roundabout.
AMERICAN TOURIST	No, it went straight there. But it was all very dangerous.
DETECTIVE	Good. Let me read this back to you to make sure I got the details straight.
AMERICAN TOURIST	Go ahead.
DETECTIVE	You're here for a fortnight on holiday and staying in a flat on the first floor. You spoke to the desk clerk and went out to the High Street for some fish-and-chips. It started to rain. You bought a brolly and came back here where you saw an unidentified man humping his suitcases down the hall whereupon he knocked over the maid, threw his baggage into a trunk which he then tossed into the boot. As he

was pulling away from the front of the hotel in his car, a lorry hit his car twice then sped away via the roundabout. Is that right?

AMERICAN TOURIST   *[Beat]* I didn't understand a word you just said.

DETECTIVE   How would you say it, then?

AMERICAN TOURIST   I'm here for two weeks on vacation and got a room upstairs on the second floor. I talked to the receptionist and went down to the main street and got some fried fish and french fries. It started to rain, so I bought an umbrella and ran back here. I then saw a man carrying his suitcase down the hall. He bumped the cleaning lady and she fell to the floor. Then he ran out to the front of the hotel, threw his suitcases into the trunk of the car and started to drive away. A truck hit him twice and then left. He drove off in the other direction. Is that clear?

DETECTIVE   *[No]* Perfectly. I'll let you know if we need any more information.

AMERICAN TOURIST   Thanks.

[They start to exit in separate direction.]

AMERICAN TOURIST   Uh... Officer...

DETECTIVE   Yes?

AMERICAN TOURIST   Can you tell me how to get to Westminster Abbey?

DETECTIVE   Do you want to go by tube?

AMERICAN TOURIST   No, thanks. I'd rather go by subway.

DETECTIVE   We don't have subways that go that far.

AMERICAN TOURIST   You don't?

DETECTIVE   No. You'll have to use the pavement.

AMERICAN TOURIST   Oh. In that case, I'll walk. Thanks anyway.

[He exits. Perplexed, the detective exits, too. Blackout. The discussion leader takes over.]

QUESTION

1. What was this sketch about and what does it have to do with anything?

13. **Formulas**

THEME
Communicating the faith.

SITUATION
An individual discusses some concerns he/she has about
modern evangelism.

CHARACTERS
Speaker

PLACE
Anywhere.

▬▬▬▬
SKIT

[Speaker is already on stage.]

SPEAKER   I don't know what to do. I keep thinking about it, but I'm stuck. See, I'm a Christian, but... I don't know how to tell other people about it. I feel restless.

I talked to my Pastor but... I don't know... everything he suggests smacks of a formula. "Four Spiritual Laws." You know what I mean. Why are Christians so obsessed with formulas? "Ten Steps To A Better Prayer Life" or "Three Steps To More Effective Evangelism" or whatever. I shouldn't be surprised, every Sunday our Pastor uses alliterated outlines. We've got to have structure and order, right?

Maybe it's just me, but I'm not sure there is a formula for our faith. I suppose there are a lot of *tools* to help us do it, but at the end of the day they're *only* tools. Sometimes they work and sometimes they don't.

It may be – and this is a wild stab in the dark – that the reason is that Christianity is about a *relationship*. And like any relationship, it has certain unchangeable consistencies – and it has a whole other part that seems ever growing and ever changing.

I don't see how it can be reduced to a formula. Where's the sense of mystery? The sense of transcendence? Even the... seduction into the beauty of Christ. Instead of mystery, we hand out paint-by-number answers. Instead of transcendence, we say that Christianity is a practical and utilitarian way to happiness. Instead of seduction, we... well, maybe there isn't an appropriate analogy for that one.

So what are we supposed to do? What are we supposed to say?

[Exits. Blackout. The discussion leader takes over.]

QUESTIONS

1. Do you agree or disagree with the speaker? Explain your answer.

2. Do you think that current approaches to the faith are handled too systematically, are too formulaic or rational? Please explain your answer.

3. If Christianity is mostly about a relationship, how can that be articulated to others?

4. Do you even agree that there is a mandate to share our faith with others? If so, how do you share your faith?

14. **Revelation**

THEME
Communicating with God.

SITUATION
The Apostle John talks to his counsellor about some strange
dreams he's having.

CHARACTERS
John
Doctor

PLACE
A counsellor's office.

▰▰▰

SKIT

[Two chairs serve as the office. The doctor enters with John.]

DOCTOR   Please, John. Sit down.

JOHN   Thank you, Doctor.

[They both sit.]

DOCTOR   You don't look so well. Is everything all right?

JOHN   I haven't been sleeping.

DOCTOR   No. Why not?

JOHN   To be honest, I've been afraid to.

DOCTOR   Afraid of sleep?

JOHN   Dreams. Bad dreams. *Really* bad dreams.

DOCTOR   Ah. *[He produces a notepad]* You better tell me about them.

JOHN   I don't know where to begin. At first, Jesus came to me.

DOCTOR   Jesus. As in: *the* Jesus?

JOHN   That's right.

DOCTOR   You were a follower of His.

JOHN   I still am. Just because I'm in exile doesn't mean –

DOCTOR   Calm down. I wasn't challenging your convictions. I was only trying to establish context. So, in these dreams, Jesus appears to you.

JOHN   Yes.

DOCTOR   Does He speak to you?

JOHN   Oh, yes. You have no idea.

DOCTOR   What about?

JOHN   Candlesticks, mostly. Messages to the various
           churches. Judgement. It's all very depressing.

DOCTOR   I can imagine.

JOHN   No you can't. No one can.

DOCTOR   What happens next?

JOHN   Well, there's a lot of doom, plagues, tribulation,
           death and horses.

DOCTOR   Horses?

JOHN   Four of them. Nasty stuff.

DOCTOR   Anything else?

JOHN   Oh – false prophets, persecution, the anti-Christ,
           Armageddon, and... let's see... the end of the world.
           That's right. The end of the world and what comes
           afterwards.

DOCTOR   Ah. What comes after?

JOHN   Another age of paradise, a final battle with Satan and
           then... life everlasting.

DOCTOR   Are these recurring dreams?

JOHN   Yes. Over and over. I think God is trying to tell me
           something.

DOCTOR   Like what?

JOHN   I'm not sure. But I've got a nagging feeling that I should do something about this. Tell somebody, maybe.

DOCTOR   Is that why you're here?

JOHN   I thought this was a good place to start.

DOCTOR   You know, of course, that dreams are the result of many different things.

JOHN   I haven't had a pizza before bed, if that's what you mean.

DOCTOR   No. I was thinking more along the lines of your subconscious – the many symbols we integrate and use in our waking life that then become reinterpreted in our sleeping life. Our minds are very complicated instruments.

JOHN   You're telling me.

DOCTOR   I think we should consider our dreams, ponder them, but don't let them ruin your life.

JOHN   The end of the civilized world as we know it is hard to ignore.

DOCTOR   But it won't really happen, John. Remember that. A dream is only a dream.

JOHN   Do you think so?

DOCTOR   Of course. Now... I can give you something to help you sleep.

JOHN   I'd rather not. Drugs make me uneasy.

DOCTOR   Okay. That's all right. There's one other thing I
          suggest...

JOHN   What?

DOCTOR   I suggest you journal this experience.

JOHN   Journal?

DOCTOR   Write down everything that happens in your dreams.
          It'll be therapeutic. Then maybe we'll be able to
          figure them out.

JOHN   I doubt it.

DOCTOR   Give it a try anyway. I mean, it's not as if anyone
          will ever see what you write. *[He stands]*

JOHN   *[He stands]* Good point. Thanks. *[Starts to exit, stops]*
          But...

DOCTOR   But what?

JOHN   What if they're real? What if God is trying to tell us
          something?

DOCTOR   *[Chuckles condescendingly]* Oh, John. You don't really
          believe that God talks to people like that any more,
          do you?

JOHN   *[Unsure]* Well... it's not unheard of.

DOCTOR   *[Dismissive]* I'll see you next week.

JOHN   Right. Next week. Goodbye, Doctor. *[Exits]*

DOCTOR   Goodbye. *[Amused]* Crazy dreams... four horses... just
          when I thought I'd heard it all... *[He gets up and
          exits.]*

[Blackout. The discussion leader takes over.]

QUESTIONS

1. Do you believe that God communicates in dreams or visions? Why or why not?

2. St John chronicled an extensive vision in the last book of Bible, commonly called Revelation. Have you ever read it? If so, what are your impressions of it? If not, what do you know about the book?

3. Many believe that the events chronicled in Revelation will one day happen as John describes them. Do you believe it? Why or why not?

4. Have you ever made an important decision based upon a dream you had? What was the dream and how did you make your decision? Did you believe the dream was a form of guidance from God? Why or why not?

15.   **Pre-emptive strike**

THEME
Conflict.

SITUATION
Adrian and Ian are discussing someone they don't like very
much.

CHARACTERS
Adrian
Ian

PLACE
Outside.

▬▬

SKIT

[Adrian and Ian enter, moving across stage on their way to somewhere. Suddenly at centre stage, Adrian stops.]

ADRIAN   Wait. There's James.

IAN   Where?

ADRIAN   Over there, by the shop.

IAN   *[Sees him]* Ah. Big deal. Just ignore him.

ADRIAN   Ignore him! How am I supposed to do that?

IAN   Easy. You walk past him without looking at him or saying anything. That usually does the trick.

ADRIAN   I can't simply ignore him. Do you know what he said – about me?

IAN   He doesn't like you, I know that much.

ADRIAN   He said he wants to beat me up.

IAN   So? You're bigger than he is.

ADRIAN   That doesn't matter. He's sneaky. He'll try to do it when I'm least expecting it. Maybe I'll go over and punch him now.

IAN   What? Why?

ADRIAN   Because he said he wants to beat me up. And I've heard rumours that he's tried to get other people to beat me up, too.

IAN   Adrian, I've known you for years. In all that time, no one has beaten you up.

ADRIAN   That's not the point. He *wants* to do it. He's tried to get others to do it. And I've also heard that he's been working out.

IAN   Working out?

ADRIAN   Getting in shape so he can beat me up.

IAN   You're kidding. Do you honestly think he cares that much about... well, beating you up?

ADRIAN   It's all he thinks about. He wants to do me in the first chance he gets.

IAN   Where are you getting all this information?

ADRIAN   Don't you worry about that. You'll have to trust me.

IAN   It sounds ridiculous to me.

ADRIAN   You say that now, but what's going to happen to you if he *does* beat me up?

IAN   What do you mean?

ADRIAN   Well, you don't think he's going to stop with just me, do you? If he takes me down, he'll go after you next. Count on it. Him and his friends.

IAN   What friends? I didn't think he had any friends.

ADRIAN   He does. Trust me. They don't like to be seen with him, but when push comes to shove – *[He pounds a fist into his hand] boom*. It's all over for you, me and people just like us.

IAN   People like *us*? What people like us?

ADRIAN   Us. *[Growls]* Look at him standing there – acting like he's done nothing wrong.

IAN   But he hasn't.

ADRIAN   But he will. Are you with me or not?

IAN   With you for what?

ADRIAN   To go knock him down. If he wants a fight, I'll give
         him a fight. Better to get him first, you know?

IAN   I'm not sure.

ADRIAN   You'd better get sure. I can't do it alone.

IAN   Let me get this straight: you wanna go beat him up
         because you're sure he's going to try to beat *you* up?

ADRIAN   Yep. I'm not only sure, I'm *certain*. Choose which side
         you're on, Ian. If you're not for me, you're against
         me. Let's go.

IAN   You mean – right now?

ADRIAN   Right now. I can't wait any longer.

IAN   Well – all right. As long as you're certain.

ADRIAN   I am. Come on.

IAN   I'm coming.

*[With clenched fists and looks of determination, they go off the
stage to "take care" of James. Blackout. The discussion leader takes
over.]*

QUESTIONS

1. What do you think this sketch is talking about?

2. How valid are Adrian's concerns about James? How would you react if you knew someone was out to hurt you? Would you take pre-emptive action against them?

3. There are nations that have Adrian's attitude – believing that other nations are out to hurt them. Are they right to take action first in the name of self-defence? Under what circumstance/s might they be right – and when might they be wrong?

16. On the motorway

THEME
The many differences between men and women.

SITUATION
A husband and wife are on the motorway together.

CHARACTERS
Jerry
Diane

PLACE
A car.

SKIT

[Two chairs. Jerry sits on the driver's side, looking very impatient. Diane approaches the car with the goodies she has just bought at the motorway service station, opens the door and gets in.]

DIANE   That's it, Jerry. Are you ready?

JERRY   *[Impatiently]* Yes! Get in, get in!

DIANE   Wait a minute. Where's your drink? I thought you wanted some coffee.

JERRY   I changed my mind. I didn't want to waste any more time.

DIANE   *Waste* time? We've been driving for three hours – I had to stop for the toilet sometime!

JERRY   Quit dawdling, will you? Close the door! *[Looks at the motorway, groans]* Oh – there goes another one!

[Jerry goes through the motions of checking the road, indicating and driving away.]

DIANE   *[Annoyed]* What's the matter with you?

JERRY   I didn't know you were going to take all afternoon.

DIANE   I was five minutes – tops!

JERRY   It doesn't matter. I'll just drive faster.

DIANE   Faster! Why? We're not late for anything. Your mother's not expecting us for hours.

JERRY   I have to catch up.

DIANE   Jerry, you're starting to worry me. Who do you have to catch up to?

JERRY   To all the cars I passed five miles back that just passed us while you were in the toilet!

[Pause/Beat.]

DIANE   *[Bewildered]* What?

JERRY   Never mind. As a woman, I wouldn't expect you to understand.

DIANE   Oh, is that the kind of conversation we're going to have?

JERRY   No. We don't need to have a conversation.

DIANE   Why not? Let's get it all out in the open.

JERRY   That's another one. Why do women always want to get things out in the open – to talk about everything? It's not as if talking fixes anything.

DIANE   Right. And why do men always feel like they have to *fix* everything? Women don't want to talk to men to get things fixed. Sometimes we simply like to share our experiences with men. It gives us a sense of togetherness.

JERRY   Why do you always need a sense of togetherness? We're together, all right? How much more of a sense of that do you need?

DIANE   Oh, right. As if you *don't* need it. What do you call your trips to the pub with all your mates?

JERRY   That's different.

DIANE   How?

JERRY   We're men. We get together to drink and watch football. It's not like we're trying to maintain a "sense of togetherness". We can sit and watch the match for hours without saying a word and *never* think: "why is he mad at me?" like you women do. We don't second-guess each other that way. If there's a problem, we say so. If we don't say so, then we assume everything's okay.

DIANE   Oh, sure. Men are all plain-speaking mean-what-you-say types. Is that it? No codes, no hidden messages.

JERRY   Yeah.

DIANE   So, when you say to me, like you did this morning: "Honey, where're my jeans?" You're not *really* saying: "Why haven't you done my laundry yet?"

JERRY   That's *your* interpretation. *[Pause/Beat]* Though they were in the laundry basket for over a week and I wanted to wear them.

DIANE   Right. You could have done the laundry yourself, you know.

JERRY   Hey, it's division of responsibility. I do what I do and you do what you do. I don't ask you to change the oil on the car, do I?

DIANE   *You* don't change the oil on the car!

JERRY   Yes, but I know how – and that's the difference.

DIANE   So the fact that I know how to use the washing machine means that I'm the one who should be responsible for the laundry? But the fact that you know how to change the oil and *don't* do it isn't sidestepping your responsibility?

JERRY   If I knew what you just said, I'd have a stunning retort. *[Pause/Beat]* Oh no.

DIANE   What's wrong?

JERRY   I took the wrong exit.

DIANE   Which exit were you supposed to take?

JERRY   I don't know – but not that one.

DIANE   Where's the map?

JERRY   I don't need a map.

DIANE   Then pull over at that petrol (gas) station and we'll ask.

JERRY   No! I'll figure it out.

DIANE   In how many miles? Don't do this, Jerry. Curb your male instinct and *ask for help*!

JERRY   But –

DIANE   *Pull over!*

JERRY   *[He pulls over]* All right, all right.

DIANE   *[Gets out off the car]* I'll be right back.

JERRY   Where are you going?

DIANE   To ask directions. Wait here.

[She exits.]

JERRY   *[Gets out]* Not a chance. *I'll* get the directions. You'll never get them right!

[Exits. Blackout. The discussion leader takes over.]

QUESTIONS

1. Do you agree or disagree with the various perspectives about men and women in this sketch? Be specific and explain your own perspective.

2. There are many clichés about how men and women behave. List as many as you can think of for men. Do the same for women. In what way/s can clichés be true? In what way/s are they untrue?

3. How can men and women use their differences to complement one another?

17. Church splits

THEME
Division in the church.

SITUATION
A talk show host chats with a guest who has personal experience with church splits.

CHARACTERS
Interviewer
Guest

PLACE
A talk show set.

SKIT

[Two chairs. A talk show.]

INTERVIEWER   … And welcome back. Our subject for discussion now is: the impact of church splits. My guest now is a man who asked to remain anonymous, but has a lot to say on the subject. *[Turns to his guest]* Good evening…

GUEST   Good evening.

INTERVIEWER   You have had a lot of experience in this area of church splits, haven't you?

GUEST   I used to be an elder [deacon, etc.] at my church.

INTERVIEWER   What happened?

GUEST   I resigned. The double life was too much for me.

INTERVIEWER   What – being an elder and a businessman?

GUEST   No – being an elder and a Christian. See, being an elder in my church was pretty dirty business.

INTERVIEWER   How?

GUEST   We were heavily involved in what some would call "religious gymnastics".

INTERVIEWER   What does that mean: "religious gymnastics"?

GUEST   Church splits.

INTERVIEWER   Uh huh.

GUEST   In the beginning, we started off as the Citywide Church of Faith, Hope & Love.

INTERVIEWER	Sounds impressive.
GUEST	But half of us got upset when the Music Director insisted on lime polyester choir robes – so we left to start our own church.
INTERVIEWER	Those doctrinal issues get 'em every time.
GUEST	Then we became the Faith Community Church of Hope & Love. But the issue of "communion" came up.
INTERVIEWER	Communion? Whether to have it or not?
GUEST	No – whether to use unsalted crackers or unleavened bread. On principle, half of us marched off to become the Neighbourhood Church of Hope & Love.
INTERVIEWER	*[Thinking about this new name]* You lost "Faith".
GUEST	Had to. Community Church took out a court injunction so we couldn't have "Faith". By this time, we didn't need it anyway.
INTERVIEWER	Then what?
GUEST	A group of us became angry when the Pastor began doing announcements at the beginning of the service instead of the traditional place before the offering was taken. So we left to become the True Believer's Assembly of Hope & Love.
INTERVIEWER	"True Believers"?
GUEST	Yes. When you get to be that small, you figure it's because the Lord was weeding out the chaff. If you know what I mean.
INTERVIEWER	Not personally. But I understand.

GUEST   Then we lost a section of our congregation
                 because they backslid and returned to Citywide
                 Church. To avoid confusion, we put up a big
                 sign saying "Under New Management" and
                 became the House Of Love – by this time we lost
                 "Hope".

INTERVIEWER   "House Of Love", huh?

GUEST   That didn't last.

INTERVIEWER   Why not?

GUEST   We had to change it because we were getting all
                 the right people – for the wrong reasons. Sailors
                 and out-of-town executives. That sort.

INTERVIEWER   But... what became of your church?

GUEST   Now it's just me. I'm the "Home Cell Of Unified
                 Saint(s)". I meet in my living room.

INTERVIEWER   Amazing.

GUEST   I had a business meeting the other night and
                 elected myself Pastor. Got a raise, too.

INTERVIEWER   That's probably the dumbest story I've ever
                 heard.

GUEST   It's as true as anything else I've told you.

INTERVIEWER   Thank you – and good night.

[Blackout (cast exits). The discussion leader takes over.]

QUESTIONS

1. Have you ever been involved in a church that suffered from a division (members leaving, perhaps to form another church)? What was the cause? How did it affect you personally?

2. List various reasons why churches split. Which one/s seem/s reasonable to you? Which ones seem petty? Explain.

3. Nearly one thousand years after Jesus Christ founded the church, it experienced its first formal split – the Western (Roman) church from the Eastern (Constantinople) church. Half a millennium later, the church was divided by the Protestant movement. Based on what you know of these historical events, would you say that the splits within the church were justified? Why or why not?

4. How do you think those outside of the church view the various scandals that tear a church apart? How would you explain the phenomenon to someone from outside the church?

Adapted from A Work In Progress *by Paul McCusker.*

18.   Interview with an old man

THEME
The elderly.

SITUATION
A talk show in which the host interviews an old man.

CHARACTERS
Interviewer
Old man

PLACE
A talk show with two chairs as the set.

▬▬▬

SKIT

[In typical talk show fashion, the host takes the stage to introduce his/her guest.]

INTERVIEWER   Hello and welcome to tonight's interview. We're honoured to have with us a genuine bonafide old man, who has agreed to come and tell us a little about what it's like to be... well... *old.* So please... welcome... our *Old Man*... Jim McCandliss.

[The old man enters, waving as he does.]

OLD MAN   Hiya. How're you doing?

INTERVIEWER   Thanks so much for joining us.

OLD MAN   Nice crowd you have here.

INTERVIEWER   Thanks.

OLD MAN   No, I mean that I know crowds and this is really a *nice* one.

INTERVIEWER   I had no idea you were an expert on crowds.

OLD MAN   Are you kidding? I used to do crowd control. At concerts and things like that. So I know a good crowd when I see one.

INTERVIEWER   What kind of crowd control?

OLD MAN   Oh, let's see... Led Zeppelin, U2, Madonna...

INTERVIEWER   What? That's impossible.

OLD MAN   I stood in front of the stage to protect her.

INTERVIEWER   Protect her? You? What did you do if someone tried to get on stage – wheeze all over them?

OLD MAN   No! They made me do that before the concert started.

INTERVIEWER   I meant that you –

OLD MAN   Hey, I was just as tough as I needed to be.

INTERVIEWER   You're making this up.

OLD MAN   I'm not! You can ask any of them.

INTERVIEWER   I'll take your word for it.

OLD MAN   I still have my backstage pass for the Madonna gig. I hung it on my rear-view mirror – the one on my wheelchair – next to the fuzzy dice – and the pine-shaped air freshener.

INTERVIEWER   Wait a minute. You have a rear-view mirror on your *wheelchair*?

OLD MAN   Of course.

INTERVIEWER   But... why?

OLD MAN   Makes it easier to change lanes.

INTERVIEWER   But why do you need a wheelchair? You're standing here – you *walked* up on stage. You look fine to me.

OLD MAN   Thank you.

INTERVIEWER   I mean that in the broadest possible sense.

OLD MAN   Where I live, wheelchairs are a status symbol.

INTERVIEWER   Where do you live?

OLD MAN   The Angelkeep Home For The Aged... and Tattoo Parlour.

INTERVIEWER	I don't believe it.
OLD MAN	You want to see my tattoo?
INTERVIEWER	No.
OLD MAN	I had one done like a birthmark so no one would know it's a tattoo.
INTERVIEWER	Then why bother?
OLD MAN	Where I live, tattoos are a status symbol.
INTERVIEWER	Tattoos... like wheelchairs.
OLD MAN	I've never seen a tattoo like a wheelchair. That's a silly idea.
INTERVIEWER	I think we lost track of where we were.
OLD MAN	We have? I was explaining about status symbols. Rest homes have hierarchies like anywhere. It's a system. A geriatric ladder of success.
INTERVIEWER	You're kidding.
OLD MAN	First we have stainless steel bedpans that double as ice trays. The beginners get those. *Then* – if you know the right people – you get extra rations of antacids. Then a nightgown that fits. And as you move up through the ranks, you'll get the better seats in the cafeteria.
INTERVIEWER	Close to the food?
OLD MAN	Close to the bathroom. That's followed by added television privileges. Next level is a leather-handled walker – with racing stripes. Finally, if you grease a few palms... the wheelchair.
INTERVIEWER	And the tattoos?

OLD MAN   You get the tattoos when you join the gang.

INTERVIEWER   A gang! You're telling me you have a *gang* at your rest home?

OLD MAN   Each ward has its own gang. Pretty nasty business. We have rumbles in physical therapy. Drive-by terrorism.

INTERVIEWER   Drive-by terrorism.

OLD MAN   Drive past very quickly in a wheelchair and throw specimen cups at the other gang.

INTERVIEWER   Look, I'm finding all this very hard to believe. Have the words "compulsive liar" ever been used to describe you?

OLD MAN   Watch your mouth. I'm old enough to beat up your father.

INTERVIEWER   So – what is the name of your gang: the Dysfunctionals?

OLD MAN   No, smarty-pants. That's the name of our rock group. The name of the gang is the Silver Streaks.

INTERVIEWER   The Silver Streaks.

OLD MAN   We wanted "The Brown Streaks" but the gang in the sample lab already had it.

INTERVIEWER   *[Trying to interrupt]* Look, no offence, but I thought we were interviewing a normal average old man. But *you*...

OLD MAN   Normal and average? What did you expect – a decrepit old fool who drools and talks about the War all day?

INTERVIEWER   I think that's what we expected, yes. Certainly not all this nonsense about Madonna and wheelchair gangs.

OLD MAN   Nonsense! Ha. You should hope to be as spry and agile as I am when you're this age. At the rate you're going, you'll live long enough to be a nuisance. I can tell. In fact, you're a nuisance *now*. You don't think growing old gracefully comes easy, do you?

INTERVIEWER   To look at you – no.

OLD MAN   It takes dignity, young man. It takes *style*. So you better start practising now.

INTERVIEWER   Thank you and goodnight. *[Guides the old man off-stage]*

OLD MAN   I'll be happy to sign autographs in the lobby.

INTERVIEWER   I'll get back to you about that.

[Exit. Blackout. The discussion leader takes over.]

QUESTIONS

1. Think through and list the expectations and characteristics you expect elderly people to have. How do those expectations and characteristics actually line up with elderly people you know?

2. Think of elderly people you know and list some of the things about them that has surprised you.

3. In general, people are living to a much older age and staying active much longer. How do you think the stereotypes about the elderly have changed over the past decade?

4. Describe how you would like to be when you reach old age.

19. **Interview with an old woman**

THEME
The essence of faith and maturity.

SITUATION
A magazine reporter interviews an elderly woman.

CHARACTERS
Reporter (could be male or female)
Mrs Shaw – a woman who claims to be one hundred years old.

PLACE
Mrs Shaw's living room.

▬▬▬
SKIT

[The Reporter enters on one side of the stage, looking around casually. Mrs Shaw, an elderly woman, enters. They clasp hands and sit down together.]

REPORTER   Thank you for seeing me, Mrs Shaw.

MRS SHAW   Sorry I'm late. I had to finish remounting the engine on my car. You're with what magazine?

REPORTER   *Christianity Monthly.*

MRS SHAW   Oh yes. I've read it. I didn't care much for that article about the role of women in the church.

REPORTER   I didn't write it.

MRS SHAW   I still didn't care for it. The Bible says what it says. Why can't you folks leave it alone?

REPORTER   I think it's a little more complex than that.

[Mrs Shaw gives him/her a steely glance.]

MRS SHAW   Physics is complex. A government bill is complex. My son's dating life is complex. The role of women in the church is not complex.

REPORTER   *[Amending the statement]* Maybe we make it more complex than it has to be.

MRS SHAW   Of course we do. We have to. How else will this generation prove how enlightened it is if it doesn't prove all the previous generations of Christians wrong? Have you ever read the writings of Augustine, Pascal, Wesley, Whitefield, Bushnell or Talmadge?

REPORTER   No.

MRS SHAW   Of course not. Nobody has. That's why they're considered classics. But you should. How else are you going to understand Christianity today if you don't understand how it developed? Did you think all we believe suddenly popped into your head during a youth pizza night?

REPORTER   *[Takes out a pocket recorder]* Mind if I record this?

MRS SHAW   If you have to.

REPORTER   You're talking about the subject of my article.

MRS SHAW   And what might that be?

REPORTER   Christianity and how it has changed over the last hundred years. You're a hundred, aren't you?

MRS SHAW   Give or take a year a decade.

REPORTER   How do you think Christianity has changed?

MRS SHAW   Christianity hasn't changed. It's the Christians who have changed.

REPORTER   How have Christians changed?

MRS SHAW   Straighter teeth, better posture. What kind of question is that? Lots of ways. Expectations. We expect too much. *[Chuckles]* That reminds me of something D.L. Moody once said. I can't remember what it was, but it reminds me that he said it.

REPORTER   What do you mean, we expect too much?

MRS SHAW   I have a shopping list. Are you sure you want to hear this?

REPORTER   Plenty of tape in the recorder.

MRS SHAW   As if that's all that counts. So, what do we expect?
We expect that there are certain rights we're
entitled to exercise – everyone wants their rights,
but nobody wants to sacrifice anything.

REPORTER   That's a broad statement.

MRS SHAW   Thank you. We expect to be committed to principle
only as long as it's convenient.

REPORTER   Christians aren't as committed as they used to be.

MRS SHAW   They're committed. But to what? There's a good
question for you. Have your magazine take a poll.

REPORTER   Anything else?

MRS SHAW   We believe we should get whatever we want
whenever we want it. It's the way of the world, you
know. Somewhere along the line we decided we're
God's chosen people and He's answerable to us. I've
looked in the Bible, I can't find it. It was different
when I was younger.

REPORTER   Better?

MRS SHAW   Not better, different.

REPORTER   How?

MRS SHAW   We had more patience. We knew how to wait – for
answers, for God, for other people to finish using
the bathroom, for the natural conclusions to our
lives. Everybody wants everything right away.

REPORTER   So, the problem is that Christians are too impatient
now?

MRS SHAW   Is that what I'm saying? Good grief, no. That's not
the problem. It's one of the problems. Another
problem is that we like to summarize our problems.

Pigeon-hole them. Put them where we can find
them. And then we pigeon-hole the answers too.
Your magazine does it every month. So, we put the
problem here and put the answer there and we
think we've solved it. Where's the faith in that?

REPORTER   So, Christians today don't have enough faith.

MRS SHAW   You're looking to get slugged with your recorder.
Don't put words in my mouth. I didn't say we don't
have enough faith. How much is enough? Is there
some kind of quota?

REPORTER   What does all that mean?

MRS SHAW   I'm telling you what it means.

REPORTER   I need you to condense it a little more. The article
can only be long enough to read in the average
quiet time.

MRS SHAW   That short, huh? So much for a debate of ideas.
Okay, here it is. I'm simply concerned that
Christians now don't allow faith time to nurture
and grow. We read all the quick-step books and use
all the catchphrases – nice on the page, they come
trippingly off the tongue, but they have little to do
with what we're experiencing. Christians are works
in progress, with faith so fragile it withers under the
harsh breath of daily struggle, yet so enduring it
blossoms under a concrete crisis. But how do you
know unless your faith comes up against it? You
can't tell how strong you are until your weaknesses
are tested. *[Leans into the recorder]* Quote that. I like
it.

REPORTER   So do I. Thank you, Mrs Shaw.

MRS SHAW   Not bad for a woman of a hundred, eh?

REPORTER   Are you really that old? Can you prove it?

MRS SHAW   You want to saw me in half and count my rings?
Go away. I'm late for my racquetball lesson.

[Blackout (Cast exits). The discussion leader takes over.]

QUESTIONS

1. What do you think of Mrs Shaw? Do you know anyone like her? In general, do you agree or disagree with her?

2. At one point, Mrs Shaw says, "We expect that there are certain rights we're entitled to exercise – everyone wants their rights, but nobody wants to sacrifice anything." Do you agree or disagree? Why or why not?

3. Respond to this statement by Mrs Shaw: "Christians now don't allow faith time to nurture and grow. We read all the quick-step books and use all the catchphrases – nice on the page, they come trippingly off the tongue, but they have little to do with what we're experiencing." Do you agree or disagree? Explain your point of view.

4. Mrs Shaw states: "Christians are works in progress, with faith so fragile it withers under the harsh breath of daily struggle, yet so enduring it blossoms under a concrete crisis. But how do you know unless your faith comes up against it? You can't tell how strong you are until your weaknesses are tested." Do you agree or disagree? Why or why not?

5. There are some who believe that the accelerated nature of our society – with instant access and immediate response to nearly everything we want – has given Christians an unrealistic expectation of how God works in and through us. What are your thoughts?

20. **The woman at the well**

THEME
Evangelism.

SITUATION
A teacher explores Jesus' method of sharing the faith.

CHARACTERS
Teacher
Reader
Jesus
Woman at the Well
Student

PLACE
A class room – consisting of a podium, centre stage, from which the teacher speaks; two chairs to serve as "the well". A few chairs off to the side could seat a few extras as students. The Reader should stand on the opposite side.

SKIT

[The teacher enters.]

TEACHER   Welcome! Our topic today is: communicating Christ
           to our world. And who better than to show us the
           right way to communicate our faith to the world
           than our Saviour Himself. Let us consider the
           encounter between Jesus and the Woman at the
           Well, as recorded in the fourth chapter of the Gospel
           of John.

[Jesus enters and sits down. Then the woman enters and also sits.]

READER   So he came to a Samaritan city called Sychar, near
           the plot of ground that Jacob had given to his son
           Joseph. Jacob's well was there, and Jesus, weary from
           his journey, was sitting by the well while his
           disciples went to town for food. It was about noon.
           A Samaritan woman came to draw water, and Jesus
           said to her:

JESUS   Give me a drink.

WOMAN   How is it that you, a Jew, ask a woman from Samaria
           to give you a drink?

TEACHER   You see? He was unconventional. A Jew asking a
           Samaritan woman for water was unthinkable.

JESUS   If you knew the gift of God, and who it is that says
           to you, "Give me a drink", you would have asked
           him, and he would have given you living water.

WOMAN   Sir, you have no bucket, and the well is deep. Where
           do you get that living water? Are you greater than
           our ancestor Jacob, who gave us the well, and with
           his sons and his flocks drank from it?

JESUS   Everyone who drinks of this water will be thirsty again, but those who drink of the water that I will give them will never be thirsty. The water that I will give will become in them a spring of water gushing up to eternal life.

TEACHER   Notice how He *intrigued* her with His statements.

WOMAN   Sir, give me this water, so that I may never be thirsty or have to keep coming here to draw water.

TEACHER   Notice that He refused her initial request for the water because it was *practical* rather than spiritual. He didn't rush to nab her conversion.

JESUS   Go, call your husband, and come back.

WOMAN   I have no husband.

JESUS   You are right in saying that you have no husband. For you have had five husbands, and the one you have now is not your husband.

TEACHER   He got to the heart of her situation by revealing truth *about her*. He engaged *her* life, her *humanity*, rather than leap straight to *His* message.

WOMAN   Sir, I see that you are a prophet. Our ancestors worshipped on this mountain, but you say that the place where people must worship is in Jerusalem.

JESUS   Woman, believe me, the hour is coming when you will worship the Father neither on this mountain nor in Jerusalem. You worship what you do not know; we worship what we know, for salvation is from the Jews. But the hour is coming, and is now here, when the true worshippers will worship the Father in spirit and truth, for the Father seeks such as these to worship him. God is spirit, and those who worship him must worship in spirit and truth.

TEACHER   He engaged her mind, her prejudices and her theology.

WOMAN   I know that the Messiah is coming. When he comes, he will proclaim all things to us.

JESUS   I am he, the one who is speaking to you.

TEACHER   *Finally* He revealed His identity to her. And then we learn what happened...

READER   Many Samaritans from that city believed in Him because of the woman's testimony.

TEACHER   There's a lot more to be said about Jesus' approach to communicating His truth. How He used stories and parables that, again, didn't lay it all on the line, but kept them wondering, thinking, searching.

STUDENT   But... Teacher...

TEACHER   Yes?

STUDENT   We don't do any of those things.

TEACHER   What do you mean?

STUDENT   We've been taught to go straight in, convince them that they're sinners and close the sale, so to speak. You know, bring them to salvation, quick and easy.

TEACHER   I see.

STUDENT   So... Jesus got it all wrong.

TEACHER   Oh. Well, it would appear so. Sorry. Thank you for coming.

[Disillusioned, everyone exits. Blackout. The discussion leader takes over.]

QUESTIONS

1. Compare the techniques of Jesus, as observed in this sketch, to current practices of evangelism. What do you think would happen if we followed His example?

2. Can you think of any other stories of Jesus that illustrate His approach to teaching those who followed Him?

21. **Going to church**

THEME
The flaws in church.

SITUATION
Two friends discuss the abandonment of one of them of attending church.

CHARACTERS
John
Michael

Note: or this conversation could take place between two women.

PLACE
A public setting.

SKIT

[John enters, pausing centre stage to check the time. Michael crosses the stage from the opposite direction and nearly passes John without noticing him.]

JOHN   Michael!

MICHAEL   Oh, hello, John.

JOHN   What a coincidence. I was just talking to Debbie about you this morning. We've been wondering what's happened to you. You haven't been to church in a while.

MICHAEL   No. I've been home.

JOHN   Have you been sick?

MICHAEL   No. Just home. You know. Doing some praying and thinking on my own.

JOHN   Oh? Has something happened? It's not like you to miss church.

MICHAEL   I'll be honest. I'm off church at the moment.

JOHN   "Off" church.

MICHAEL   Yeah. You know. I've had it up to *here* with the hypocrisy.

JOHN   Oh.

MICHAEL   You know what I'm talking about. The church is a place where things are supposed to be different. People are supposed to love one another. That's not what I see at our church. We've got gossip, pettiness, jealousy... you name it.

JOHN   You mean you're upset because the people at church
            are acting like... people.

MICHAEL   They're going to have to do a little better than that
            if they want me to get out of bed and go there. I get
            enough of people at my job, if you know what I
            mean.

JOHN   So you don't think the people at church should be
            like people?

MICHAEL   Of course they're people. But they're supposed to be
            Christians. And that means being different from just
            people. They're supposed to love one another and be
            committed and pray and show joy
            and... and... make me feel glad I'm there.

JOHN   So... what you're looking for is the perfect church.

MICHAEL   In a way, I suppose.

JOHN   But there's only one problem with that.

MICHAEL   What?

JOHN   The minute you join the perfect church, it won't be
            perfect anymore. See you later. *[He exits]*

MICHAEL   *[Pauses to think about it]* What do you mean by that?
            John? *[Follows John off]* Just what are you saying to
            me?

[Exits. Blackout. The discussion leader takes over.]

QUESTIONS

1. Describe what you would consider to be the perfect church.
   Do you think such a church exists?

2. Describe what you would consider to be the most common
   problems in a church. How do you react to those problems?
   How can those problems be fixed?

3. Have you ever given up on going to church? Why? What
   did it take (or would it take) to get you to return?

4. How do you think most people view the church – positively
   or negatively? What do you think puts most people off
   church?

5. It has been said that the church is a hospital for sinners, not
   a museum for saints. Do you agree with that statement? Do
   you think some people have unrealistic expectations about
   how church people should behave? How do you respond to
   the accusation that the church is full of hypocrites?

22.   **Whose music?**

THEME
The generation gap.

SITUATION
A teen seeks out a compact disc from his or her father.

CHARACTERS
Teen (could be a son or a daughter)
Father (could be adapted to a mother)

PLACE
A living room.

SKIT

[Father enters with a stack of mail, absent-mindedly flipping through the envelopes as he makes his way across the stage. Teen enters.]

TEEN   Dad, where's my Supergrunt CD?

DAD   It's in my car.

TEEN   What's it doing there?

DAD   I was listening to it on the drive to work.

TEEN   But it's *my* CD. Why are you always taking *my* CDs?

DAD   Always? I don't always take your CDs.

TEEN   Yes, you do. Why can't you leave my stuff alone?

DAD   Look, I'm sorry. What's the problem here?

TEEN   You're messing everything up. You're supposed to have your music and I'm supposed to have mine.

DAD   But I like your music.

TEEN   No, no, no. You're not allowed to like my music.

DAD   Says who?

TEEN   It's the way it's supposed to be. Don't you understand? My music is... well, *mine*. And yours is yours. That's what separates us – our generations. Get it? I want my own identity so I listen to music I like. And it wrecks everything if you like my music, too.

DAD   I had no idea it was so complicated. I... like your music. That's all. I didn't think it would throw you into a crisis.

TEEN   Well, it has. It's thrown all of us into a crisis.

DAD   All of you?

TEEN   All my friends. Their parents are doing the same thing – listening to their stuff. It's... it's unnerving.

DAD   All right. I'm sorry. The disc is in my car. I won't borrow it again.

TEEN   Thanks. *[Starts to go]*

DAD   Son?

TEEN   Yeah?

DAD   Since we're sorting out our inventory... Can I have my Abba disc back now?

TEEN   *[Exasperated]* Dad! *[Storms off stage]*

[Father shrugs and exits. Blackout. The discussion leader takes over.]

QUESTIONS

1. Do you think there is there a "generation gap" between parents and children? If so, how does it manifest itself?

2. Do you think young people want their own identities – one that is distinct from their parents, their tastes and their enjoyments? Explain your answer.

23. **Giving**

THEME
Giving.

SITUATION
In which a couple discusses increasing their giving to the church and uncovers a deeper problem.

CHARACTERS
Bob – the husband. Annoyed with the Pastor's sermon about giving.
Vicki – the wife. Seriously considering the idea of giving more money to their church.

PLACE
Their living room (as simple or as elaborate as you care to make it). Two chairs centre stage would certainly be enough.

▬▬▬

SKIT

[Two chairs centre stage. Bob and Vicki enter – having just arrived from church. Bob is obviously agitated – almost comically so. Vicki is preoccupied with a chequebook she is scrutinizing. Bob is speaking as he enters.]

BOB   *[Moving to TV downstage and mimes turning it on as he speaks]* Give, give, give. He held us up fifteen minutes extra with another message about giving. I'll bet I missed half of the match because he couldn't get off his... his tirade... *[Looks at TV, gestures to it]* You see? I missed the first half. The man is obviously not a football fan. Why do preachers feel compelled to do that?

VICKI   He doesn't do it that often. In fact, I can't remember the last time he talked about giving. Why are you so annoyed?

BOB   Because everyone wants our money, that's why. The charities on the telly, in the magazines and newspapers, the letters in the post – they all want a piece of my bank account. I'm tired of it. *[Sits down to watch TV]*

VICKI   You're just mad because you missed a little bit of the football game.

BOB   A little bit? The first half, thank you. If a man wants my money, it's not advisable for him to make me miss the match.

VICKI   What about God?

BOB   He understands the necessity of football.

VICKI   Will you stop talking about football, please? I think we need to talk about our giving.

BOB   You talk, I'll listen.

VICKI   It doesn't work that way *[Moves to TV]*.

BOB   *[Sees her move, watches her anxiously knowing full well what she is going to do]* Wait. Don't. We'll talk. *[She turns it off]* She turned the TV off. *[Puts face in hands]* It's a conspiracy. She's in on it, too. *[Looks up at her as if she has his undivided attention]* Giving. Right. I'm ready to have a meaningful dialogue.

VICKI   *[Sits next to him]* Good. I think we should consider increasing what we've been giving.

BOB   Increasing? *[Stands and moves away as he speaks]* What do we increase? Time? Between the two of us we're at the church every night. That doesn't count Saturday mornings, Sunday services, and afternoons.

VICKI   I'm talking about money.

BOB   So am I. What price do we put on our time?

VICKI   I didn't know we were supposed to do that.

BOB   Maybe we should start. Everybody else does. Did you know that John and Brenda hardly give to the church at all? They figure they give their fair share in time. If we followed that rule, the church would have to give us refunds.

VICKI   That's John and Brenda. *[Pause/Beat]* I thought we were doing it as a matter of personal conviction.

BOB   We are. But maybe we're too... convicted.

VICKI   You're not serious. I've been looking through our bank statement and – well, do you realize we're not even giving ten per cent of what we bring in?

BOB   Since when is ten per cent a magic number?

VICKI   It's mentioned in the Bible.

BOB   Literally or figuratively? We give what we can afford.

VICKI Can we afford *not* to give at least ten per cent?

BOB You and the Pastor are obviously in cahoots. Look, we're tight financially. Your new car and my golf clubs didn't come cheap. Not to mention the other things we buy to keep us happy in the lifestyle to which we've become accustomed.

VICKI But, Bob –

BOB Do you want to take over the finances? Go ahead. They're yours.

VICKI That's not what I'm saying. This has nothing to do with your ability to handle our finances.

BOB Then why are we talking about this?

VICKI Because I was affected by what Pastor said this morning. We should consider giving more than we have been.

BOB And whose pocket will it come out of? Are you willing to tighten up more – cut back on clothes, shoes, nights out after choir practice?

VICKI If you're willing to cut back on golf, the racquet club, and stereo equipment, then yes, I am.

BOB *[Laughs with disbelief]* We'll see.

[Long pause.]

VICKI This idea wasn't supposed to be a tug-of-war. *[Shakes her head, confused]* I don't know what's happening here. I always believed that we gave from our hearts together – not on strict budgetary guidelines. *[Pauses, stands, takes a step towards Bob then stops]* Do you remember when we first accepted Christ? It was right after we got married. We were in that little apartment and you worked at that dry-cleaning place. I was working – where was I working?

BOB *[Half-smiles]* Some diner. Leo's or something.

VICKI   That's right. My feet still hurt just thinking about it. You used to pick me up and we'd have devotions over a cup of coffee. Remember? *[Pause/Beat]* We didn't have much money but I know we gave a lot more than ten per cent. Percentages didn't matter then.

BOB   We were new Christians.

VICKI   And we were giving to the Lord. Out of love for Him.

BOB   *[Slow to admit it]* I remember.

VICKI   But here we are now in an "upper-middle-class tax bracket" and we can't afford to give like we used to. *[Pause]* Maybe God needs to take back what He's given to us so we can. *[He provides no reaction, she sighs]* Go back to your ball game. I'm finished. *[She turns and exits]*

BOB   *[Almost as a delayed reaction, he calls after her]* Vicki... Vic... I'm just trying to be... *[Regular tone, almost to himself]* practical. *[Thoughtful pause]* It's certainly not like it used to be. *[Sadly]* I wonder why that is. *[He frowns and slowly turns away... Exits]*

[Blackout. The discussion leader takes over.]

QUESTIONS

1. The overall implications of a sketch such as this can prove to be very complicated. In general, what do you think the key message is (if you think one can be found)?

2. Speaking honestly, who are you inclined to side with, Bob or Vicki? Why? If you think you can see both sides, what points do you agree with? What do you disagree with?

3. If you were able to advise Bob and Vicki, how would you suggest they deal with this conflict?

4. Reference 2 Corinthians 9:7. How does it shed light on this subject?

24. The retirement

THEME
Goodbyes.

SITUATION
A retiring Vicar says farewell.

CHARACTERS
Reverend John Haworth
Margaret – his secretary

PLACE
The Vicar's office.

SKIT

[Reverend John Haworth enters his church office. There is a small table off to the side. On the top, a box is surrounded with books waiting to be packed. He looks around the office, sighs, then moves to the table and slowly – meticulously – packs the books. He continues this as Margaret, his secretary, enters.]

MARGARET   John – your wife called while you were out and said to meet her at the hotel. The movers finished at the vicarage (parsonage) and it's all locked up.

REVEREND   Thank you, Margaret.

MARGARET   Do you realize how late it is? You can finish that packing tomorrow.

REVEREND   I'll only be another minute.

MARGARET   Don't strain your back.

REVEREND   *[Pleasantly]* Margaret, you're a nag.

MARGARET   I'll miss you, too.

[This stops him for a moment. He pauses, then goes back to work.]

REVEREND   It's hard to believe I'm retiring.

MARGARET   What will you do?

REVEREND   I don't know. Perhaps I'll finally get to read all those books I never got to read.

MARGARET   Like what?

REVEREND   Leviticus, Malachi, Revelation…

MARGARET   You taught a class on Revelation.

REVEREND   I know. I made it all up. With all that symbolism – who could tell? *[He stops, leans on the desk wearily]* I'm tired.

MARGARET   Why don't you go home?

REVEREND   I can't. They locked it up.

MARGARET   Then go to the hotel.

REVEREND   I will. Don't rush me.

[Pause – Haworth looks around, lost in his thoughts.]

MARGARET   What are you thinking about?

REVEREND   Everything. The joy, the frustrations of the job... I made so many mistakes here. I may never know how serious some of them were.

MARGARET   But you did a lot of good. One day you'll see the fruits of those labours.

REVEREND   That's what's important, I suppose.

MARGARET   What do you remember the most?

REVEREND   Oh, heavens. I don't know. *[Looking around]* This place is full of memories. Not only mine. It's four hundred years old. It has permanent shadows on the wall . *[Pause/Beat]* I wonder where mine are? I wish – *[Stops himself, pause]*

MARGARET   What do you wish?

REVEREND   That's a bad game to play: "I wish".

MARGARET   What would you like, John? What do you wish more than anything?

REVEREND   To be remembered. *[Pause/Beat]* Goodnight,
Margaret. Close everything up, will you?

MARGARET   Yes, sir. And get a good night's sleep.

REVEREND   Stop nagging me. I will. *[Moves to exit, turns to her]*
Thanks for everything. *[He smiles at her, then exits.
She watches him a moment, considers the office once
more then moves to exit.]*

MARGARET   It'll never be the same without you. *[Looks around]*
But it never changes, either.

[Exits. Blackout. The discussion leader takes over.]

QUESTIONS

1. Imagine yourself saying goodbye to a place, even a life,
you've always known. How do you think you'd feel? What
kinds of memories might come to mind? What kinds of
regrets?

2. Think of your life now – the places you go, the people you
know. What would you change if you could? What would
you say to the people you know if you weren't going to see
them again? What would you change in your relationships
with them?

3. If you could retire now, how would you spend your time?

Adapted from The Pearly Gates *by Paul McCusker.*

25. Healing

THEME
Faith and Healing.

SITUATION
While getting ready for a funeral, a young girl and her brother react to a television faith healer.

CHARACTERS
Television evangelist
Elizabeth
Mark

PLACE
A family room.

SKIT

[Lights up. Elizabeth is sitting on the couch watching TV. We do not see the screen, but we hear the sound: a TV evangelist. Elizabeth is dressed nicely, as if she's going to church.]

TV EVANGELIST   TV... that's the problem. Christians today just don't know what they want from God. He says "Ask and you'll receive" and we're not asking! Why aren't we asking? Because we don't believe! We're afraid to ask! Well, I don't know about your Bible, but *my* Bible says to "ask and you'll receive"! Ask! What do you want from God? What do you want? Answer that question then ask God for it. Whatever it is, he'll give it to you. This is what Satan wants to keep from you. This is the power he wants to yank out of your hands. Ask and you'll receive. You want healing? Ask for it! Someone you love sick and dying? Ask for their healing! God'll give it to you! I've spoken with Him... I know it from His word! Look beyond your unbelief, He says, and keep your eyes on me for I am the author and finisher of your faith and if you'll stay in faith and keep your eyes upon me I will perfect that which concerns thee and I will finish thy faith and you will see the reality of what you believe me for coming to pass in thy life if you'll stay in faith and don't let the Evil One steal my word out of thy life. *[Pause/heavy breathing]* Call the number at the bottom of the screen and let me know what you want, and I'll take it to God for you. Health? New Car? Healing? Marriage restored? Eyesight? Money? Call now. Our prayer line is open. And don't forget that miracle gift of $100 or $50 or $1000 because it tells the Lord you believe what He's saying through this ministry. Ask – and you'll receive. Anything –

[During the onslaught of faith, Mark enters and waits quietly next to Elizabeth. Elizabeth looks up sadly. He waits expectantly. she picks up the remote control and turns the TV off.]

MARK   Everyone's in the car. Are you ready? *[Pause]* Elizabeth?

[Elizabeth nods and stands up. She adjusts her dress. She is close to tears.]

ELIZABETH   I didn't have anything to wear for a funeral. Is this too bright?

MARK   You can wear whatever you want.

ELIZABETH   You don't think it's too... too much? They dressed Dad in his best suit. He'll look good. Like he did for church.

MARK   Don't worry about it. You look fine.

ELIZABETH   Okay. Did you hear that man – on the television?

MARK   A little bit.

ELIZABETH   Maybe we didn't have enough faith, huh?

[He doesn't answer. She begins to cry and exits past him.]

MARK   *[Looking at the TV]* Maybe we didn't send in enough money.

[Exits. Blackout. The discussion leader takes over.]

QUESTIONS

1. What do you think of the concept of supernatural healing? Do you believe that God always heals people of their illnesses? Explain your answers.

2. Do you believe that God sometimes *won't* heal people because of a lack of faith – on their parts, or on the parts of others? Why or why not?

3. How did you feel while listening to the television evangelist? Do you agree or disagree with him? Why?

Adapted from A Work in Progress *by Paul McCusker.*

26. **God told me**

THEME
Hearing God.

SITUATION
Two young people talking.

CHARACTERS
First Person
Second Person

Note: could be any combination of male or female.

PLACE
Outside a cinema.

SKIT

[Our two characters enter as if they are just leaving a cinema (though the audience won't know that).]

FIRST PERSON	Yes, there's no question in my mind. God told me to do it.
SECOND PERSON	How do you know?
FIRST PERSON	What do you mean: how do I know? He told me.
SECOND PERSON	But how did He tell you?
FIRST PERSON	He just... *told* me.
SECOND PERSON	But *how*? Did He whisper in your ear? Did you hear a clap of thunder?
FIRST PERSON	Don't be stupid. God doesn't communicate that way – well, not very often.
SECOND PERSON	Then how? How do you know God was talking to you?
FIRST PERSON	I felt it in *here*. *[Taps chest]* I felt Him saying to me that I should do it.
SECOND PERSON	So it wasn't physical or audible or anything like that. It was a feeling.
FIRST PERSON	Yeah – a feeling.
SECOND PERSON	How do you know it wasn't just that?
FIRST PERSON	Just what?
SECOND PERSON	A feeling. Like I sometimes have feelings that are just... feelings. They aren't God telling me

to do anything. I just *feel* like doing it – so I do. How do you know?

FIRST PERSON   You can tell the difference.

SECOND PERSON   *How?*

FIRST PERSON   You just do. I don't know. You pray, you read your Bible, you stay in tune with the Holy Spirit. Then you know. The feeling is there and you know.

SECOND PERSON   Amazing. I don't think God has ever talked to me like that.

FIRST PERSON   He will. I'm sure He will. Maybe when you get a little more mature – you know, in your faith.

SECOND PERSON   I guess so. *[Pause/Beat]* Though I think you're going to have a hard time convincing Mrs Hammersmith about it.

FIRST PERSON   What do you mean?

SECOND PERSON   *[Gesturing back towards the way they had come]* I don't think she's going to believe that God told you to come and see a movie rather than go to school today.

FIRST PERSON   Hey, she can't blame me. God said to do it – so I did.

[Exit. Blackout. The discussion leader takes over.]

QUESTIONS

1. The Bible is full of stories about people who heard God speak and responded to it – sometimes when it didn't make sense to those around them. Do you believe that God speaks to people today? If so, how?

2. Has God ever spoken to you? If so, how did He speak and what did He communicate to you?

3. In what ways can we be certain that God is speaking to us – and that we aren't victims of our own feelings, desires or rationalizations?

4. There was a time when it was commonly believed that God spoke only through His Church (and its leadership) and not through individuals by their own authority. By what authority can we ever claim that God speaks through us?

27. Life on the Box

THEME
The influence of television.

SITUATION
An individual ponders his life decisions based on what he learned from television.

CHARACTER
Speaker (could be male or female)

PLACE
Anywhere.

━━━

SKIT

[Our Speaker enters.]

SPEAKER So... I can't figure out what's gone wrong. I mean, it works so well for those characters on television that I thought, well, why not? Why can't I live like they do? They're all so clever and funny and, yeah, they get into scrapes, but even *those* are funny. Why not live my life like that? Never work. Just hang out at one of those coffee cafe places and meet good-looking people and say witty things and try to discover who I am and maybe meet someone I fancy and sleep with her and hang out some more and be... well... happy. *They* sure are. *[Pause/Beat]* But I ran into problems almost right away. Without a job, I couldn't afford the coffee in those places. And very few good-looking people came in and even the ones that did wouldn't talk to me. And, you know, it's *very* hard to say witty things all the time. And when I met someone I fancied, I either put her off because she didn't fancy me back – or she thought I was throwing myself at her or, in the case of someone I met a few weeks ago, we had a deliriously exciting night together and then... well, they never get pregnant on these shows, do they? I guess they got abortions. I don't know. But that wouldn't be very funny, would it? I didn't think so. Or if they do get pregnant on those shows, then they wind up playing out some comical situation with the baby. I don't know how they do it. Babies cry a lot and have to be fed and the nappy has to be changed and... it's not very funny, really. *[Pause/Beat]* I'm really disappointed. I feel like these shows make promises they can't really keep. Shame, they were some of my favourites. *[Pause]* So you can imagine my surprise when I woke up one morning and realized that I'd been living the wrong life. Strange, huh?

[Exits. Blackout. The discussion leader takes over.]

QUESTIONS

1. How do you think television programmes and movies
   influence the way we think and act?

2. Do you think most television programmes have a positive
   or negative influence on our society? Explain your answer.

3. What do you consider the best programme on television
   now? What do you consider the worst? Explain your
   choices.

4. Do any of your favourite programme actually present ideas
   and messages contrary to your own point of view? If so,
   how do you reconcile what they present versus your own
   belief?

28. **Too many programmes, too many courses**

THEME
Involvement.

SITUATION
In which an average person speaks his mind about too many
church programmes and courses.

CHARACTERS
Percival Sniffhounder – a true man of the people (in other
words, use your imagination).
Announcer – an off-stage, "television" voice.

PLACE
A TV studio (implied).

━━━

SKIT

[As our commentator walks on stage, the Announcer announces...]

ANNOUNCER   And now *Speak Up* – an editorial comment from a local viewer.

PERCIVAL SNIFFHOUNDER

[In position, looks straight ahead "into the camera"] Good evening. My name is Percival Sniffhounder and I want to speak out against overzealous churches. I have been a Christian my entire life – born into the church, properly baptized and a regular attender on all major holidays. That is certainly more than enough to keep a man on the proper path to a good life. But lately I've been disturbed to see churches that were solidly grounded in the great traditions of discreet inactivity now abandoning them for bothersome and unnecessary involvement. It seems now that a day doesn't go by when I'm not being nagged and cajoled into attending this function or contributing to that function or reaching out to yet another somebody-or-other. It's most off-putting.

[Pause/Beat] They tell me it's to help me grow in my faith. Since when have we ever expected the church to do that? They say it's to make me a *better* Christian. Better in what way, I ask? Is it not relative? Is it not enough that I insist on my wife giving to the altar guild? I believe we are going from the sublime to the ridiculous.

[Holds up a church bulletin] By way of example, I offer you this church bulletin. Look it over for yourself. It's chock-a-block of all kinds of absurd things. *[Opens the programme]* Classes and studies and... *[Points]* Look at this. A class about *evangelism*! When in heaven's name did the church succumb to this crass form

of proselytizing? What will people think of Christianity if it carries on so?

No, I don't like this trend. I don't like it at all. It's yet another attempt to make us feel that we are not good enough as we are. And I, for one, happen to think we're perfectly acceptable – certainly no better or worse than the next person. No, you can keep all your extra-curricular classes to yourself. It's what's wrong with our country today.

[Pause/Beat] Well, that's my opinion. And I think I speak for more than myself when I offer it. Thank you. *[He exits]*

ANNOUNCER   This has been *Speak Up*. Responsible replies are encouraged. The viewpoint expressed here is not representative of this station or any intelligent human being. Thank you.

[Blackout. The discussion leader takes over.]

QUESTIONS

1. Do you agree or disagree with Mr Sniffhounder's viewpoint? Why or why not?

2. What kinds of programmes or courses does your church have? Do you think they have enough or should they develop more? If more, in what areas?

3. Do you think some churches offer too many programmes and additional courses?

29. The calling

THEME
Knowing God's calling.

SITUATION
David (or Donna) relates a personal story.

CHARACTERS
David (or Donna)

PLACE
Anywhere.

SKIT

[David (or Donna) is already on stage.]

DAVID   I've been singing at my church for five or six years now. At first I did it because they needed me to. We don't have a lot of very good singers at our church, if you know I mean. Then, after a while, people kept saying that I was good. Really good. A friend of mine said he had some equipment at home, for recording, and told me to go over and record some songs. So I did. He burned a few discs for me. People who heard the recordings said I had a lot of talent – a lot of them said I was *gifted*, that I have a calling to sing, to use my voice for God. Full-time. As a ministry. I sang for other churches. Then they were saying that I should broaden my ministry. You know, get a record company. So I tried. I even recorded some of the songs in different styles. You know: pop, rock, rap, hip hop, country and western – just to show my versatility. I even won an award at one of the Christian festivals and got a lot of acclaim at the Christian camps. I was invited to a seminar, one of those talent competitions, where they teach about talent and then give you a chance to show to a lot of real record company executives what the Lord is doing in my life. With my talent, that is. My gifts. *[Pause/Beat]* I was up against a woman who did a reggae gospel version of "Amazing Grace" and a Madonna lookalike who did "Shine, Jesus, Shine". *[Pause/Beat]* He was pretty good. *[Pause/Beat]* So I sang my heart out for the judges – vice-presidents and executives of various record companies and music publishers. It was my big moment. *[Pause]* They looked bored. One kept fiddling with his watch. But I won. I even got to sing again for everyone at the conference. They put me on last. It was midnight and nearly everyone had gone home by then. But I sang my song. Then I went home and waited for the calls. They didn't come. I work as a clerk at Safeway now.

[Pause]
I wish I could figure out why God called me to a full-time career as a Christian singing star – and won't give me an audience. Don't get me wrong, I'll do what He wants me to do. But... I wonder about it sometimes.

[Exits. Blackout. The discussion leader takes over.]

QUESTIONS

1. Do you believe that people are "called" by God to do things? If so, how are people called? What might they be called to do?

2. David (Donna) clearly believes that he/she is called by God to sing full-time. Yet circumstances seem to be working against that belief. Is David (Donna) wrong about his/her calling? Or is David (Donna) expected to be more patient with God?

3. It's interesting to note how many people believe they are "called" to talents, gifts, or occupations that are public in nature – glamorous or "star"-like. Yet, how many people do you know who profess to being "called" to mundane activities?

4. Do you believe that you are "called" to do anything? If so, what? How do you know for sure?

5. What are effective ways to "discern" your talents, abilities, gifts or "calling" – and to know if you should pursue them in a full-time capacity?

Adapted from A Work In Progress *by Paul McCusker.*

30. **The chair**

THEME
Knowing God's will.

SITUATION
An individual contemplates discerning God's will.

CHARACTERS
An individual (could be male or female)

PLACE
Anywhere.

▬▬▬▬

SKIT

[Individual is already on stage.]

INDIVIDUAL   I can't move. I want to, but I can't. I'm not sure
if it's God's will. I've prayed about it, sure. I've
searched the Bible. I've sought the counsel of
respected Christian leaders. But no one can say
for sure that it's God's will for me to move. My
common sense tells me it's all right. I *feel* like
moving, too. But can I trust my common sense?
Can you trust emotions? *[Pause/Beat]* Sometimes I
think of all the things I could do for God if I
moved. But then I think it might be Satan
tempting me to act out of pride. So I stay put.
[Pause/Beat] Maybe God is trying to teach me a
lesson. What does He want me to learn from this
experience? I wonder. *[Pause/Beat]* There are a lot
of times in my life when I think God is trying to
instruct me. I'm never sure *what* He's teaching
me, though. Either I'm a terrible student – or
He's not a very good teacher. That's not really
what I meant to say. I'm only trying to sort out
why He doesn't make it a little clearer about
getting out of this chair. A still small voice would
be nice. Even a loud scream. But I don't hear
anything. And I don't have enough confidence
to move on my own. Why doesn't He do
something to make His will absolutely clear? It
wouldn't be so hard, would it, Lord? Just a sign.
A hint. I won't move until You say so. Use my
mind... my heart... my very spirit to reveal
Yourself to me. They're open to You – if you want
me out of this chair.
[PAUSE.]
I have to go to the bathroom.

[Exits. Blackout. The discussion leader takes over.]

QUESTIONS

1. Can you empathize with the person in this sketch? If so, in what way/s?

2. How would you define the term "God's will"? Have you ever wondered what it is God wants from you – or what He wants you to do? If so, how have you sorted out the answer?

3. Do you believe that God communicates His will to people? If so, in what way/s?

4. If God has a specific desire for you, do you believe that you have a choice about whether or not to obey that will – or will He accomplish what He wants in spite of your choice?

Adapted from A Work In Progress *by Paul McCusker.*

31. Honestly

THEME
Living truthfully.

SITUATION
An individual confesses.

CHARACTERS
Fiona (or could be a male)

PLACE
Anywhere.

SKIT

[Our character enters.]

FIONA   I'm ashamed of myself. I really am. I was in our Bible
          study – you know what I mean. Just a group of us who
          get together to talk and pray. And we started talking
          about our lives. And everyone was so... well, in
          control. Everyone seemed to have their lives and their
          faith in place. I was tempted to go along with them. I
          could have lied. That's always been the easiest thing to
          do. As long as I'm behaving properly – going to
          church, keeping involved, participating in socially
          acceptable activities with my Christian friends –
          nobody needs to know what's going on inside of me.
          I'm accepted. What's wrong with that? I want to be
          accepted. It's us against the world. Simple, right?
          [Pause/Beat] But the world I'm supposed to be against is
          the one I live in. It's full of my friends who *aren't*
          Christians. People I care about. Oh, they respect my
          beliefs... as long as I don't bring them up. That suits
          me. They would only feel uncomfortable if I tried to
          explain – and they wouldn't understand anyway.
          [Pause/Beat] So I'm accepted. In both groups. In both
          worlds. But never at the same time. And I wonder – do
          other Christians feel like this? Probably not. I'm the
          only one. *[Pause/Beat]* I'm just trying to be honest. I
          mean, I look around at other Christians and –
          sometimes I think we're just plain weird.

[Exits. Blackout. The discussion leader takes over.]

▬▬▬

QUESTIONS

1. Have you ever felt like this character? In what way/s?

2. Do you ever put on an act of feeling something you don't feel, or believing something you don't believe, simply to be accepted by others? If yes, what do you think would happen if you confessed what you were really feeling or believing?

3. Do you ever think that other Christians are "just plain weird"? If so, in what way/s?

4. The phrase "be in the world, but not of it" is often tossed around in Christian circles. What do you think it means? How can we be in the world, but not of it?

Adapted from A Work in Progress *by Paul McCusker.*

32. So...what's wrong with it?

THEME
Lust.

SITUATION
Jane and Terry have an argument about a certain type of men's magazine.

CHARACTERS
Jane
Terry

PLACE
Outside a shop that sells magazines.

▬▬▬

SKIT

[Jane makes a beeline across the stage, obviously upset. Terry is close on her heels.]

TERRY   Jane – wait. *[Grabs her arm] Wait! [She turns to look at him defiantly]* What's wrong with you?

JANE   What do you mean – what's wrong? I can't stand those magazines – *you* looking at those magazines.

TERRY   What magazines? What are you talking about?

JANE   You know. The one with the blonde on the front – the blonde with hardly any clothes on.

TERRY   *[Dismissive]* Oh, that. Look, it had an article in it about a new band that I like –

JANE   Yeah, sure. No doubt the editors put a lot of time in the quality of their *writing* for a magazine like that.

TERRY   They do. The articles are very good.

[She looks at him sceptically.]

TERRY   I hardly noticed the girl on the cover. I saw the headline. The one about the band I like. So I picked it up. Besides, what's wrong with it having an attractive woman on the cover?

JANE   What's wrong? You want to know what's *wrong*?

TERRY   I asked you first.

JANE   For one thing, she wasn't wearing any clothes to speak of.

TERRY   So? She has a beautiful body. Why not let people appreciate it?

JANE   *Appreciate!* I have a hard time believing that you look at a girl like that and merely "appreciate" her.

TERRY   What are you implying?

JANE   I'm talking about *lust*, Terry. Are you saying you don't lust after someone like that?

TERRY   Depends on what you mean by "lust".

JANE   You want a definition from a dictionary? You know what it is.

TERRY   Okay, so maybe I lust occasionally. What about it?

JANE   It's wrong.

TERRY   What's wrong with it? It's something that happens in my mind, that's all. It's how men are wired. It doesn't hurt anybody. I mean, it's not like I'm going to go out and rape someone just because I see a picture of a sexy girl.

JANE   That's not the point, is it?

TERRY   Then what's the point?

JANE   It's what lust does to you – to *us*.

TERRY   You've lost me completely now. What does it do to me – or us?

JANE   When you lust after a girl like that, it creates a fantasy – it makes a promise that it can never fulfill with an object that isn't real.

TERRY   Still lost. You better go on.

JANE   That girl isn't real. She's just an object for you to lust after. There's no intimacy, no human connection, you can lust after her and move on as if love, sex and relationships are… are disposable.

TERRY   But –

JANE   Wait. And she creates an expectation that no one can fulfill. I certainly can't. How am I supposed to compete with that airbrushed model who has parts that defy gravity and probably spends most of her time working to keep it that way. I can't. I'm lucky to get fifteen minutes on the exercise bike. How can I match that? And how can I be sure that when you're with me, you're not imagining her?

TERRY   *[Pause, then:]* Are you always this serious on a first date?

JANE   I'll see myself home, thanks. Nice to meet you. *[She exits]*

TERRY   *[Calls after her]* Then I guess I can forget that kiss goodnight.

[Terry follows Jane off the stage. Blackout. The discussion leader takes the stage.]

QUESTIONS

1. How would you define lust? Do you agree with Jane's opinions about lust? Why or why not?

2. Terry dismissed part of Jane's concerns about lust by saying it's how he's "wired". Is that true? Is lust all right as long as no one "gets hurt" by it? Is there anything men can do to control their lust?

3. Do you believe there's a positive or negative impact on men, women and our culture by allowing scantily-clad women to appear on easily-seen magazine covers, television or movies? Explain your answer.

33. The mid-life crisis

THEME
Mid-life crisis.

SITUATION
In which three kids try to determine what to do about their parents' mid-life crises.

CHARACTERS
Scott – late teens, very "dry" sense of humour.
Aimee – mid-teens, very practical.
Cara – pre-teen, a bit precocious.
Jan – the mother (and subject of part of the conversation).
Dave – the father (and also subject of part of the conversation).

PLACE
A family room.

▬

SKIT

[Scott, Aimee and Cara enter. We should get the feeling they're "up to something". Aimee is carrying a book (explained in play dialogue). They are all anxious for Aimee to get the book open so it can answer their burning questions. Their conversation begins as they are entering. They then huddle themselves around the book.]

SCOTT   Aimee – quit messing around. Is that the book?

AIMEE   Keep your voice down. It's one of them.

SCOTT   Is it the right one?

AIMEE   I don't know. They have so many. This one was the easiest to grab before Mum walked in.

CARA   You better hurry. They'll be down any minute.

SCOTT   I hope it's the right one.

AIMEE   It should be. *[Reading the front]* Dr Jameson Answers Questions About What Parents Wish Their Children Knew About Husbands And Wives. *[She looks for the chapter they want]*

SCOTT   You need three volumes just for the title.

CARA   Are there any pictures?

AIMEE   It's not *that* kind of book, Cara.

SCOTT   It doesn't have pictures? I'm surprised Dad bought it.

AIMEE   *[Finding the right chapter]* Here we go… "Mid-Life Crisis". *[Pause/Beat]* Do we want to know about women or men's crisis?

CARA   You mean there are two different kinds?

SCOTT   We're in bigger trouble than we thought.

AIMEE   *[Reading]* "Women..." *[Pause/Beat]* Oh. They call it
          "menopause".

CARA   *Men*opause for women? What is it for men:
          *Girl*opause?

SCOTT   Go to your room, Cara.

CARA   No way. They're my parents, too.

AIMEE   Are you listening to this or not? It says here that
          menopause is a physical and emotional transition
          women go through when they end their reproductive
          capacity.

CARA   So *that's* what it is! I could've told you that.

SCOTT   That explains why Mum cries every time she sees a
          baby.

AIMEE   Yep. It lists the symptoms...

CARA   *[Her attention is drawn off-stage]* Wait, I think she's
          coming.

AIMEE   *[Engrossed in book, not hearing]* Extreme emotional
          shifts from joy...

JAN   *[Entering, pleasant]* Oh, look! It's so nice to see you
          kids playing together.

AIMEE   To depression...

JAN   It's going to be so difficult when... *[Suddenly weeping]*
          when you leave home!!!!

SCOTT   Yep. You can check that one off.

AIMEE   Low self-esteem.

JAN   *[Still crying]* If only I'd been a better mother…

SCOTT   Check.

[Without looking away from the book, Cara hands her Mum a tissue. Jan takes it and gives her nose a good blow.]

AIMEE   Unpredictable outbursts of anger for no apparent reason.

JAN   *[Exploding]* Well, don't just sit there! Isn't anyone going to ask me what's wrong?!? Doesn't anyone around here *care* that I'm crying?

SCOTT   *[To Jan]* We care, Mum. *[To Aimee]* Check that one off, too.

AIMEE   Let's see… *[Continues]* Inappropriate emotional responses.

JAN   *[Beginning to cry again]* Oh… you children are so good to me. You make me so… so… *[Wailing]* happy!

SCOTT   *[Nods to Aimee, gestures to book]* Uh huh. That gets it.

AIMEE   Forgetfulness…

JAN   *[Abruptly]* Where's your father?

CARA   He's upstairs getting dressed, Mom.

JAN   Oh?

AIMEE   An unreasonable suspicion that there is a rival for the spouse's love.

JAN   *[Suspiciously]* Why is he getting dressed? Is he going somewhere?

CARA   He's going out tonight.

JAN   He *is*? With whom? Where is she?

CARA   She's *you*, Mum. You two are going out together.

SCOTT   *[Referring to book]* Bingo on those.

JAN   *[Working up to more tears]* Really? Oh, that thoughtful, thoughtful man!! *[She weeps again and exits]*

SCOTT   Boy, Mum's a walking case study.

AIMEE   Oh, I forgot one...

SCOTT   What?

JAN   *[Screaming from off-stage]* Keep the ruckus down in there! Are you trying to disturb the whole neighbourhood?

AIMEE   A low tolerance to noise.

SCOTT   Of course.

CARA   What are we going to do? Is there a cure?

AIMEE   *[Searching the book]* It doesn't say.

SCOTT   A lot of help this Doctor is, whoever they are.

CARA   What about Dad? What's it say about him?

AIMEE   "Mid-Life Crisis in Men..." Lessee... "the first and most obvious hint that a man is going through mid-life crisis may be found in his appearance."

[Dave now enters in full mid-life crisis gear. He should be remminiscent of John Travolta in Saturday Night Fever. *Shirt unbuttoned to navel... gold chains... very contemporary hairstyle which is completely inappropriate to the man himself... polyester trousers... coloured shoes to match his belt... and any other*

adornments you may decide upon. Dave is bright and outgoing, too cool for words.]

DAVE   Hey, dudes! What are your righteous selves doing huddled around a book on a Friday night? Like, it's party time!

CARA   Dad? Is that you?

SCOTT   There *better* be a cure for this.

DAVE   Of course it's me! Where's that bodacious babe I'm going out with tonight? I don't wanna be late for the mosh-pit dance contest at the Pink Jackhammer Club downtown. *[Very cool, jive-like]* And I do mean *downtown.*

CARA   Maybe we should have him put to sleep.

DAVE   *[Puts on sunglasses]* Hey, Scott, you do me right and I'll let you pull the Jag around front for me.

SCOTT   Jag? What Jag?

DAVE   The Jaguar I bought this afternoon.

SCOTT   *[Shocked, to Aimee]* Is that in the book?

AIMEE   Yeah... status-symbol materialism.

DAVE   *[Tosses keys to Scott]* And don't get any dirt on the genuine artificial leather sheepskin seat covers.

SCOTT   In a Jag? *[to Aimee]* Is there anything in there about an extreme lapse in taste?

AIMEE   Just look at him and you know the answer.

JAN   *[Entering]* Nobody move. I have an announcement to make.

DAVE   Hey, like *radical*. I dig announcements. Reminds me
          of school.

SCOTT   *[To Aimee]* Is that – ?

AIMEE   Trying to recapture his lost youth, yes.

JAN   Dave… children… *[Pause/Beat]* I'm going to have a
          baby.

[Pause/Beat.]

DAVE   Cool!

SCOTT   *[Calmly]* No you're not, Mum.

JAN   I *want* to have a baby, then.

DAVE   Bogus!

SCOTT   *[Calmly]* You can't, Mum. It's out of the question.

JAN   Can't I even think about it? I want a baby-waby so
          bad. They're so cute…

DAVE   Yeah!

SCOTT   No. Your body-wody has said byey-wyey to baby-
          wabies. *[To Aimee]* You better show her the book,
          Aimee.

DAVE   A book? Does it have pictures?

JAN   *[The tears are coming]* I don't care what that book says.
          I want a baby and I want it now.

SCOTT   Sorry, Mum.

CARA   *[To Aimee]* You better show her the section about how
          long it takes to make babies, too.

160 52 Instant Skits

JAN   *[Crying]* But I want a baby.

SCOTT   It's all right, Mum. You have *us*.

[Instantly, the three kids pose and smile angelically at their parents.]

[Pause/Beat.]

JAN   Oh no... *[She wails and runs off the stage]*

DAVE   Like, what's the reaction here? I thought we were, like, headed for an excellent party, you know? *[He follows Jan]* Hold the lachrymal fluid, my little push-pin of passion! *[Turns to kids]* You kids are, like, major bummers. *[Exits]*

CARA   Did any of you understand what he just said?

SCOTT   How long is this going to last?

CARA   Yeah. Parents just aren't what they used to be.

AIMEE   *[Searching book]* There's a small section here about dealing with parents in mid-life crisis.

SCOTT   Yeah? What's it say?

AIMEE   Only four words.

SCOTT   What?

AIMEE   Four words. "Head for the hills".

[The three of them look at each other as if the idea is a good one.]

ALL TOGETHER
            Righteous, dude!

[They run off the stage. Blackout. The discussion leader takes over.]

QUESTIONS

1. Have you ever had to cope with parents who have gone through a dramatic change in their attitudes or behaviour? What was behind the change? How did you cope?

2. What do you know about "mid-life crises"? Have you or anyone you know ever had to deal with one? How did it manifest itself? What was the outcome?

3. We often expect or desire our parents to stay constant and consistent – even while complaining that we wish they would change. How realistic are our expectations and desires? How can we be more understanding of our parents and what they might be going through?

With much appreciation to the Williamson family.

34. **Protection**

THEME
Orthodoxy.

SITUATION
In which a government agent gives some surprising news to a "conservative" Christian.

CHARACTERS
Zucker – a "conservative" Christian.
Floyd Jackle – a government agent, dressed in overcoat, dark sunglasses and carrying a clipboard.

PLACE
Zucker's living room.

SKIT

[Zucker and Jackle enter. As they talk, Zucker is looking at Jackle's business card, gestures for Jackle to sit down. He does. Zucker also sits.]

ZUCKER   You're Floyd Jackle with what government agency?

JACKLE   The Office of Wildlife Protection. Or, the Wildlife Protection Office. Mind if we sit down?

ZUCKER   No, go right ahead. *[They both sit down]* If you're looking for a contribution, I'm not really int –

JACKLE   No, no, no. That's not why I'm here at all.

ZUCKER   Then what can I do for you? I'm not a hunter.

JACKLE   I just need to double-check my information. You're Ralph – *[Looks at clipboard]* Ralph D. Zucker. Correct?

ZUCKER   Yes.

JACKLE   And you believe that the Bible is the inspired, inerrant Word of God?

ZUCKER   Yes.

JACKLE   And Jesus Christ was born of a virgin, performed literal miracles, raised people from the dead, was crucified for your sins and Himself rose from the dead three days later?

ZUCKER   Yes. He is God incarnate.

JACKLE   "God incarnate." Yes, I'll add that. *[Scribbles it down]*

ZUCKER   What is this?

JACKLE   You believe in the Genesis account of creation?

ZUCKER   Yes.

JACKLE   And Jesus is the *only* way to get to heaven – not one
         of many different ways?

ZUCKER   Right.

JACKLE   A person cannot get to heaven by good works.

ZUCKER   No, a person cannot.

JACKLE   Hell is a literal place of punishment for those who do
         not accept Christ?

ZUCKER   It is.

JACKLE   Heaven and eternal life await believers after death.
         Literally.

ZUCKER   Literally, yes.

JACKLE   And Jesus Christ will return literally and physically to
         earth one day.

ZUCKER   He will.

JACKLE   *[Stands]* You do not smoke, drink, chew tobacco, cuss,
         dance, or go to movies with more than a "G" rating?

ZUCKER   No, I don't.

JACKLE   Well, sir, under Ordinance 215701264-51784, you are
         entitled to protection as an Endangered Species
         because of the rarity of your habitat and lifestyle. If
         you ever feel endangered, just call the number under
         my name on that card. Good day, sir. *[He exits quickly]*

ZUCKER   *[Still sitting, dumbfounded, looks at the card with
         disbelief, long pause]* This is a joke, isn't it? *[Stands,
         follows to exit]* Someone put you up to this, didn't
         they? Hey! *[Exits]*

[Blackout. The discussion leader takes over.]

QUESTIONS

1. As absurd as this sketch is, in what ways are Christians becoming a minority (or an endangered species)?

2. Do you think Christians are becoming unusual or irrelevant to our modern times? Explain your answers.

Adapted from The Pearly Gates *by Paul McCusker.*

35. Dramatic conversions

THEME
Outward Appearances.

SITUATION
In which two girls become Christians – but with two very different results.

CHARACTERS
Carole – a girl who becomes a Christian with great emotion.
Cindy – another girl who becomes a Christian quietly.
Brian – one of a crowd of excited Christans.
Crowd – several extras who serve as excited believers.

PLACE
It could be anywhere a group of people might meet.

SKIT

[A crowd enters, with Carole at the centre. Carole is weeping and talking. They are off to the side, towards stage right.]

CAROLE   … and I've done some terrible things…

ONE MEMBER OF THE CROWD
        Like what?

CAROLE   Terrible, terrible things. Too hideous and shameful to talk about.

SECOND MEMBER OF THE CROWD
        Tell us just a couple of details. One or two.

CAROLE   No… it's all over now. Jesus is my Lord and Saviour now. My life is completely changed.

[Affirmative "oohs" and "aahs" from the crowd.]

CAROLE   I'm sorry I'm crying but I'm overwhelmed with the joy of the Lord.

[More "oohs" and "aahs" and gestures of comfort from the crowd.]

CAROLE   *[Being encouraged by the crowd's interest, speaks more boldly]* Jesus Christ has washed me in His blood and I'm completely giving my life to Him. I'm giving up smoking, drinking, drugs, rock'n'roll, and… *[At a loss for something else to give up]* designer sunglasses!

[Again, "oohs" and "aahs" from the crowd.]

CAROLE   And though I just became a Christian, I know God's will is that I become the wife of a Pastor one day.

[The crowd "oohs" and "aahs" even more. They begin hugging Carole and each other, surrounding her completely, and miming

*conversation. Cindy enters stage left, sees the crowd, moves to Brian
– who is on the fringe – and taps on his shoulder.]*

BRIAN   *[Turning to her]* Hi, Cindy. *[Keeps looking at crowd,
hoping not to miss anything.]*

CINDY   What's going on?

BRIAN   Carole became a Christian at church tonight. *[His
answer is direct – obviously trying to put her off so he can
get back to the crowd]*

CINDY   I know. *[Humbly]* So did I.

*[Brian didn't hear because he turned back to the crowd. Cindy taps
him on the shoulder again.]*

BRIAN   *[Impatiently]* What?

CINDY   *[Smiling]* I said I became a Christian tonight, too.

BRIAN   *[Still not hearing]* That's nice. *[Concentrates on crowd]*

CINDY   *[Perplexed, taps Brian on the shoulder again, he turns]*
Jesus Christ. I accepted Him tonight. Carole and I
did it at the same time.

BRIAN   *[Surprised and suspicious]* You did? Are you sure?

CINDY   Yes, I am. *[Puzzled]* Why?

BRIAN   You're not crying.

CINDY   Crying?

CAROLE   *[Shouting to crowd]* Come on, I'll show you the very
spot where I made the decision. The exact spot!
*[Carole and the crowd exits stage right. Brian watches
them, even takes a step or two in their direction, yearning
to follow]*

CINDY   *[Tugging his arm]* I don't understand. What do you mean about crying?

BRIAN   If you just became a Christian you should be crying.

CINDY   But I'm happy.

BRIAN   Weeping for joy. Like Carole. If He really changed your life you'd be crying.

CINDY   But He hasn't changed my life yet. It just happened. Without making me cry.

BRIAN   When Jesus Christ takes over a person's life, it should be dramatic.

CINDY   Dramatic?

BRIAN   Yes, extremely. Are you giving up cigarettes and liquor?

CINDY   I never smoked and I don't drink very often. Is that part of it?

BRIAN   Of course! What about drugs? Sex? Rock'n'roll?

CINDY   No drugs, little opportunity for sex so that's not an issue, and I prefer classical music.

BRIAN   *[Impatiently]* Designer sunglasses?

CINDY   Couldn't afford them.

BRIAN   *[Shaking his head sadly]* I don't know about this. I mean, I hate to put it this way but… well, your salvation seems to be a dud. Look at Carole – she's a good example of salvation. She even knows that God's will is for her to become the wife of a Pastor. Do you know God's will for your life?

CINDY   I thought I'd take it day by day and let Him reveal it to me through prayer and Bible study.

BRIAN   No offence, Cindy, but I think you need to go back and try it again.

CINDY   Try it again?

BRIAN   Absolutely. If you've really become a Christian, then you'll show it. A few tears would help. See you later. *[He exits stage left, shaking his head sadly]*

CINDY   *[Stands, shocked, repeats Brian's words thoughtfully]* Maybe I was wrong. Maybe it didn't happen after all. Oh well... *[Looking bewildered, she exits...]*

[Blackout. The discussion leader takes over.]

QUESTIONS

1. What is the experience of "conversion" – what does it involve? What feelings, if any, accompany it? When you became a Christian, what feelings did you experience? Among those you know, are there any common feelings shared at the time of conversion or is each person's experience unique? Reference 1 Samuel 16:7. How might that verse apply?

2. Is there any indication from the Bible about the conversion experience and how a person should behave? Look through the Gospels and look at the reactions of those who encountered Christ: should we expect people to behave the same way now? Are we fair to expect anything at all (in terms of reaction) from a person who has just become a Christian?

36. Instant Christianity

THEME
Patience with spiritual growth.

SITUATION
We hear an advertisement for Instant Christianity.

CHARACTERS
Advertisement announcer

PLACE
Anywhere.

___

SKIT

[Announcer is already on stage.]

ANNOUNCER   You don't like to wait in long bank lines, so they created cashpoint machines. You want something to eat in the middle of the night? 24-hour restaurants and grocery stores! Do you have physical pain? Take a drug and relief comes fast, fast, fast. It's what you expect – it's what you enjoy. That's why Mercenary Television Products is proud to present... Instant Christian! The new, automatic way to arrive in the faith. Just a little Instant Christian and those prayers will be answered when you *want* them answered – those nagging verses from the Bible will become clear as glass – and those troublesome personality quirks will simply disappear! *[Pause/Beat]* Is sin a problem? – Not for Instant Christian! A quick application and they're gone in record time! What about conflicts with other Christians? Don't worry! Instant Christian will eliminate them before you can say "thorn in the flesh". And you don't have to worry about those unsightly grey areas, either. Just use Instant Christian and everything will turn to black and white! It's fast, easy – and you won't have to think about it! And you can use Instant Christian anywhere! At home, at church, in your Bible Studies – even on the golf course on Sunday mornings! It's simple to apply and requires no additional application. Instant Christian – because in this modern world, who has time to wait for change? Available at our 24-hour freephone order desk or in all fine chemists everywhere.

[Blackout (Announcer exits). The discussion leader takes over.]

QUESTIONS

1. The Christian life has often been equated with a journey – a lifelong process of faith and growth. Yet, in this age of instant gratification, how do you think the lifelong process of faith has been affected?

2. Because we can get what we want so quickly and easily, do you think we have developed unrealistic expectations of God? Have we developed unrealistic expectations of ourselves?

3. Have you ever wished that those nagging doubts and sins in your life could simply vanish through a pill? Do you think we sometimes pray in the hope that God will act like a miracle pill and make our problems go away?

4. What does the Bible say about the Christian life – discipleship – and the end result of a life of faith?

Adapted from A Work In Progress *by Paul McCusker.*

37. **The date**

THEME
The perception of Christianity.

SITUATION
A girl warns her parent about the boy she has a date with.

CHARACTERS
Dad
Mum
Daughter

Note: with slight adjustment to dialogue, Daughter could be
Son.

PLACE
A family room at home.

SKIT

[Dad and Mum are sitting. Dad is reading the newspaper. Mum is trying to finish darning a sock. Karen enters, dressed to go out and looking apprehensive.]

DAUGHTER   Mum, Dad... I want to talk to you before Brian gets here.

DAD   Why? What's wrong?

MUM   Who's Brian?

DAUGHTER   The boy I'm going out with tonight.

MUM   Oh, him.

DAD   Brian who?

DAUGHTER   Brian Fitzgerald. You haven't met him, Dad. You're going to meet him tonight.

DAD   What's wrong with him?

DAUGHTER   What makes you think something's wrong with him?

DAD   Because you want to talk to us before he gets here. What's wrong with him? He's not going to be like that... that Joe bloke you went out with?

MUM   Oh dear.

DAD   So many body piercings he looked like he'd been riveted together.

DAUGHTER   Brian isn't anything like that.

DAD   He's like that... what's his name?

MUM   Which what's his name?

DAD   The one I didn't like.

DAUGHTER   You don't like any of them.

DAD   But the one that I especially didn't like. With the funny... whatchacallit on his... you know.

DAUGHTER   Oh *him*. No. Brian doesn't have anything like that.

DAD   Good. So what's he have?

DAUGHTER   What do you mean?

DAD   Why are we talking about him and missing the *Six O'Clock News*?

DAUGHTER   Because I want you to know about Brian. He's unlike anybody I've ever dated.

DAD   We established that.

MUM   Did we?

DAD   Yes. Now get on with it.

DAUGHTER   Brian is... a Christian.

MUM   A Christian?

DAD   I'm missing the *News* for that bit of information?

DAUGHTER   When I say he's a Christian, I don't mean that he's a Christian like us.

DAD   How can he be a Christian and not be like us?

DAUGHTER   For one thing, he goes to church every Sunday – not just Easter and Christmas.

DAD   You're joking.

MUM   Is he a fanatic?

DAUGHTER   He's... dedicated to his faith.

DAD   A fanatic.

MUM   Oh dear.

DAUGHTER   What I mean is... He prays and reads his Bible
            and –

DAD   Reads his Bible? What does he think that'll get
            him?

DAUGHTER   A lot of things, I suppose.

DAD   I don't like the sound of this. People who read the
            Bible are weird – they think God is talking to
            them. *Personally.*

DAUGHTER   Maybe He is.

DAD   Don't you start.

DAUGHTER   I'm not. Look, I like him. He's... kind and
            gentlemanly and bright and funny and
            intelligent... and it's refreshing to meet someone
            who really believes in something.

DAD   Now wait a minute. I believe in something. Don't
            I, Doris?

MUM   Yes, George.

DAUGHTER   Like what?

DAD   I believe in... in... lots of things. Too many to
            mention. I don't like the sound of this boy. He
            isn't even here and he's causing trouble already.

DAUGHTER   He's not causing trouble.

DAD   He's a fanatic – they always cause trouble. They're so intense and... and make you feel guilty for things you haven't done.

MUM   Or you did once but got over it.

DAUGHTER   That's right. It's embarrassing and uncomfortable.

MUM   Oh dear. I don't like the sound of this at all.

[There is a knock at the door off-stage.]

DAUGHTER   That's him. Now... be nice. Please!

[The daughter runs to answer it.]

MUM   Come on, George. We have to be nice.

DAD   I think I liked what's-his-name with the whatchacallit better. At least you knew that *he* didn't believe in anything that made you feel embarrassed and uncomfortable.

[Blackout (Cast exits). The discussion leader takes over.]

QUESTIONS

1. Do you think that we, as a society, now view Christianity as a negative rather than a positive? Explain your answer.

2. If Christianity is now perceived as a negative, what do you think has brought it to this point?

3. In some places, one's seriousness about one's faith is often viewed as a form of fanaticism. How do you think it's viewed within your circle of friends and family?

38.   **The marathon runners (a parable)**

THEME
Perseverance.

SITUATION
In which two runners conflict over continuing the race they're in.

CHARACTERS
First Runner – wants to stay in the race.
Second Runner – thinks that it's time to stop.

PLACE
Possibly a park. A bench is all that is needed.

SKIT

*[Two runners enter stage right. Runner number two stops at the
bench, breathing heavily, sits down. Runner number one realizes
that number two has stopped. Turns back.]*

RUNNER ONE	What are you doing?
RUNNER TWO	Stopping.
RUNNER ONE	What?
RUNNER TWO	This looks like a good place to stop. I want to stop now.
RUNNER ONE	We can't stop. We have to keep going.
RUNNER TWO	We don't have to. Don't you like it here?
RUNNER ONE	*[Looks around]* It's very nice.
RUNNER TWO	There. See? It's a good place to stop. You should be glad that we've made it this far.
RUNNER ONE	I am. But –
RUNNER TWO	We've come a long way. *[Stands – looks right]* Wow, look how far. It's great. We should be proud of ourselves.
RUNNER ONE	We didn't do it alone.
RUNNER TWO	No. Of course we didn't. But we did do it. *[Shakes head with amazement]* It seems like yesterday that we started. It's hard to believe so much time has gone by. So many memories.
RUNNER ONE	*[Tugs at Two's arm, moves left]* Yes. We can talk about them as we go. I don't think it's healthy for us to stop now.

RUNNER TWO   Sure, it's healthy. *[Points right]* Will you look at what we've accomplished? We should celebrate. This is a landmark – a milestone! *[Looks harder]* I can hardly see where we began.

RUNNER ONE   Let's go.

RUNNER TWO   You know what I'm thinking? *[Sits down again]* I'm thinking that maybe we should stop here for good. Why do any more? We could stop now and feel very proud about how far we've come. We've made it a lot further than others have.

RUNNER ONE   That's no reason to stop. We're just starting to get momentum.

RUNNER TWO   You're kidding. Aren't you even a little tired?

RUNNER ONE   No! I feel like we just left. I want to keep going.

RUNNER TWO   Why? What's the point?

RUNNER ONE   I want to get to the finish line. It's why we got in this race to begin with. Remember?

RUNNER TWO   *[Leans, looks left]* I don't see any finish line.

RUNNER ONE   *[Looks left]* I do.

RUNNER TWO   *[Stands, looks left]* Where? I don't see it.

RUNNER ONE   *[Points to head]* Here. *[Points to heart]* And here.

RUNNER TWO   *[Sits again]* Cute. That's cute. I'm mean for real.

RUNNER ONE   That is for real. At least, it was when we started. You saw it at the beginning. It's what kept us going – a clear vision of that finish line.

RUNNER TWO   Well... that was when we started. I don't know now...

RUNNER ONE   Come on, let's go. If you start to move, it'll come back to you.

RUNNER TWO   But this is such a good place to stop. *[Gestures to the right]* Remember those runners we passed a little way back? They stopped and they seemed happy.

RUNNER ONE   That's their business. Don't you remember how they were walking? They were arthritic. Their muscles were atrophied. Their joints were stiffening. It'll happen to you.

RUNNER TWO   But... but you don't know what's ahead! It could be dangerous. There could be big pits to fall into or mountains to climb!

RUNNER ONE   We knew that when we started. We jumped over the holes, we climbed the mountains. Our faith got us through.

RUNNER TWO   It's too much. It's too much to ask us to do!

RUNNER ONE   Not compared to the One who went ahead of us. We're travelling light. He had a load on His back.

RUNNER TWO   He was special. I'm only human. It's... it's too risky.

RUNNER ONE   No riskier than when we started! But we had faith. The same faith that got us this far will take us the rest of the way. I'm going now. Are you coming?

[Long pause, Runner Two looks left, then right.]

RUNNER TWO   Nah. Go on. Maybe I'll catch up with you later.

RUNNER ONE   I doubt it.

RUNNER TWO   I think I'll go back and see what those other guys are doing. They stopped and they seem to be doing just fine.

RUNNER ONE   Are you sure?

RUNNER TWO   Yes, I am.

RUNNER ONE   I'm sorry. I think you're making a big mistake. You're going to miss out on so much. *[Moves left]* Take care. *[Jogs off left to exit]*

RUNNER TWO   Bye. *[To himself]* Fanatic. *[Slowly, stiffly, he stands]* Oh… *[He tries to limber up but it only shows how much he has stiffened already]* Guess I sat there too long. *[Shouts right as he hobbles]* Hey guys! What are you doing? *[He hobbles – exits right]*

[Blackout. The discussion leader takes over.]

▬▬▬▬▬▬

QUESTIONS

1. In some ways, this sketch could be considered a "parable". What is the point of this sketch? What is the race the two runners are in? Do you agree with the first or second runner? Why? Why do you disagree with the other?

2. In what situations could this sketch – and its point – be applied to in your own life? Be applied to in your church?

3. Reference 1 Corinthians 9:24–27; 2 Timothy 4:7–8. How do they apply to this sketch?

39.   The hypochondriac

THEME
Prayer.

SITUATION
A monologue in which we hear a Christian explain the
problems with his prayer life.

CHARACTERS
Hypochondriac

Note: could be male or female, with appropriate adjustments.

PLACE
A home.

SKIT

[Hypochondriac is already on stage.]

HYPOCHONDRIAC   My Christian therapist called me a hypochondriac this morning. He said I suffer from an abnormal anxiety over my spiritual health and inflict upon myself spiritual conditions that are imaginary. I was wounded by the observation. I can't imagine what caused him to lash out at me so unfairly. I think it's because I don't pray for him enough. I really should – and often feel bad that I forget.

That's the problem. My prayer-life, I mean. When I pray, I go through my mental checklist, usually starting with my wife (we have no children, so I pray about that), my mother and father, then moving chronologically through my family – all my brothers and sisters and their families – and then my wife's family – all her brothers and sisters and their families – and then our immediate friends and their families – and then my co-workers and their families – and by that time I'm so tired that I forget to pray for the peripheral people in my life like my Christian therapist.

It makes me heartsick to think about all the people whose lives might be more closely attuned to the will of God, who would be in the firm hollow of His hand, if only I'd prayed for them more often.

It's my fault, I know. I can't seem to concentrate when I pray.

For example, the other night, after my wife had gone to bed, I decided to finish reading the day-by-day devotional book I've been using for the past three years. It's a guidebook for spiritual empowerment –

containing quotes from all the great
Christian classics by authors like Billy
Graham, the Pope, the Archbishop of
Canterbury and Chuck Colson. Most people
finish it in a year. It's taken me three years
because I start every January 1st , stop
reading around January 12th, then try to
catch up on all the readings I'd missed until
around January 18th, when I give up again.
Then I read haphazardly for about a fraction
of the rest of the year whenever I think to
feel guilty about it. So this year I decided to
forget the dates and read it all the way
through just like a regular book and, as I
said, was just finishing it up the other night.

Anyway, I was determined to finish this
book and the devotional for December 31st
was by Philip Yancey, I think, and he was
talking about "praying in" the New Year.
Since it was the middle of June I felt a little
strange doing it, but poor Philip didn't
know that when he wrote it, nor could I
have anticipated reading it at the wrong
time of year. I went ahead to give it a try.

Dear Father –

As I began to pray I thought of a song I'd
heard on the radio that day. I tried to make
it stop and couldn't. I tried to think of
another song and couldn't. I imagined
myself pushing a big red "Stop" button as if
turning it off – but it wouldn't stop. I tried
praying louder in my brain, virtually
shouting at God, but it only made my head
hurt. I then forced myself to relax. Maybe it
would go away by itself. I took several deep
breaths. The song seemed to recede, or at
least the volume got turned down, and I
started to pray again.

Dear Father –

For no particular reason I suddenly
wondered if I'd remembered to give a

particular file to my boss at work. It wasn't an important file. Just something she'd asked for on Friday. Did I give it to her?

Oh, and if I didn't, I should remember to put the previous quarter's sales figures in it. She'll want to see those.

Maybe I'd better write a note to myself to do that on Monday.

I started to write the note on a scrap piece of paper when I remembered that I was supposed to be praying. After hastily scribbling the note, I went back to my prayer.

The song I'd heard on the radio came back again. I'd never thought of the radio as a tool of Satan, but now I was.

I started to feel a little impatient.

Dear Father – I prayed quickly, thinking that if I slipped it in fast enough, I'd trick my brain into going along with me. It then came to my mind that I'd forgotten to call my mother this past week. I should do that tomorrow, I thought. I made a note on my scrap piece of paper.

My devotional book taunted me. I hadn't really prayed yet. I had managed "Dear Father" and that was all. Why was I under attack like this? Why couldn't I get my mind under control?

I began to think about that. Was my spiritual life so shallow that I couldn't even pray for a few minutes without distraction? What was wrong with me?

In the midst of trying to answer those questions, I realized that I was still thinking and *not* praying. At the rate I was going, I really would be praying in the New Year with Philip Yancey.

New Year. What did my wife and I do for New Year's Eve last year? I wondered. Were we with my brother's family – or was that the year before? We'd done something at church, maybe? No. We stayed home and watched a movie. That's right. We had wanted a quiet New Year's Eve at home. And then I remembered that I was supposed to be praying.

I threw the devotional book across the room.

Wrestled and pinned to the mat of spiritual failure, I gave up and decided to "pray in" the New Year – some time next year.

[Exits. Blackout. The discussion leader takes over.]

QUESTIONS

1. Can you sympathize with our "Hypochondriac"? If so, how?

2. What do you think is an effective way to pray?

3. When do you think is the best time of day to pray? The best place?

4. Do you think that prayer is a matter of spontaneity or a matter of discipline?

5. What does the Bible say about prayer and the best ways to do it?

40. **Executive decisions**

THEME
The price of success.

SITUATION
A man is promoted – and loses more than his old office.

CHARACTERS
James
Barbara

PLACE
An executive office.

SKIT

[Barbara enters. She looks sad but determined. She has something on her mind. James enters – knowing what's coming but wanting to sidestep it somehow.]

JAMES   Barbara? What are you doing down here? The party's in my office. Well, my *new* office. *[With mock pride]* You should see it. I'm on the fifth floor. It has a view.

BARBARA   It's wonderful for you, James. Congratulations. You'll make a wonderful vice-president, I'm sure.

JAMES   I'm so glad you came. I thought you wouldn't. *[He pulls an envelope from his pocket]* Did you see this? Mr MacPherson gave it to me right after his speech. It's a bonus.

BARBARA   James –

JAMES   We could take a nice holiday (vacation) with this. We'll have time now. I finally made it, Barbara. After all those years of working... slaving... I made it. Now we'll have time for that holiday (vacation) we've talked about.

BARBARA   It's too late for a holiday (vacation), James. You know that.

JAMES   Too late? No. It's never too late.

BARBARA   It is for me. Please, James, I thought we were going to keep it simple.

JAMES   Simple! How can we keep it simple? You're leaving me. How could you expect that to be kept simple? *[With resolve]* We can make it work, Barbara. Things have settled down now. I've made it. I'm here.

BARBARA   You don't believe that any more than I do.

JAMES   But I do! I can make more time now.

BARBARA   How? You think that as a vice-president they'll let
            you have more time? They won't. You have more
            responsibilities now.

JAMES   This time it'll be different.

BARBARA   That's what you said when they made you a district
            manager. And again when you were promoted to
            head of sales. And again when – *[Pause/Beat]* Oh,
            what's the point. It's an old conversation.

JAMES   I can give you more time, Barbara. I promise.

BARBARA   *[Sighs]* I don't want any more of your time, James.

JAMES   Then what *do* you want? What is it?

BARBARA   I don't want anything.

JAMES   Look, I know it's been difficult – sitting on the side
            while I paved out a career. But it wasn't just for me.
            It was for *us*. And... and I'm there!

BARBARA   Yes... there.

JAMES   What do you want? Tell me.

BARBARA   Nothing.

JAMES   I can't accept that. There must be –

BARBARA   James, I... I don't love you anymore. The love isn't
            there. I feel – I don't feel anything.

JAMES   *[Surprised]* Nothing at all?

BARBARA   You better go back to your party.

JAMES   You know this is a mistake. A big mistake.

BARBARA   Maybe – but I'm not going to think about it.

JAMES   We could get help. There are things we can do – people we can talk to – if you want to try.

BARBARA   I'm beyond trying. Your life will go on fine without me. Just as it did when you were with me.

JAMES   There are details we have to work out.

BARBARA   Our lawyers can work them out.

JAMES   You have a lawyer?

BARBARA   Yes. Goodbye, James. And... congratulations. *[She exits]*

JAMES   *[Calling after her]* Barbara. Barbara!

[James follows Barbara off the stage. Blackout. The discussion leader takes over.]

QUESTIONS

1. What is your impression of the couple in this sketch? Describe how you imagine their life together until now.

2. Barbara doesn't seem to believe James when he says he'll have more time for them. Do you believe him? Why or why not? Do you think he believes himself? Explain your answer.

3. Is Barbara right to leave James now? Why or why not?

41. **Promises**

THEME
Priorities.

SITUATION
A man is too busy to spend time with his family.

CHARACTERS
Geoff
Veronica

PLACE
A home office.

▬▬▬
SKIT

[Geoff is sitting at a desk, working diligently on some reports.]

VERONICA   *[Entering]* Geoff?

GEOFF   *[Without looking up]* Hm?

VERONICA   The children are ready – and so am I. Are you coming?

GEOFF   *[Looks at watch]* I can't, Veronica. I simply have to get this done.

VERONICA   But you promised. You said we'd all go to the zoo today. Together.

GEOFF   I know... but I didn't know that David would dump this on my lap before he left on holiday (vacation). Go on without me. We'll all do something together on another day.

VERONICA   That's what you said when you bowed out of going to the park last week.

GEOFF   I'm sure the children understand.

VERONICA   Do they?

GEOFF   They'll *have* to. It's not like I'm only their father. I have responsibilities. My time is not my own. They *have* to understand that – or get used to it.

VERONICA   Yes... of course. It's only that...

GEOFF   Only what?

VERONICA   It's only that you promised. And if a Vicar can't keep a promise, then who can?

[Pause.]

GEOFF   I'm sorry. Just... explain it to them, will you?

VERONICA   Of course. There's a fresh pot of tea in the kitchen. We'll see you later then.

[Veronica turns and exits. Geoff goes back to work – stops – then throws his pen down onto the desk and speaks (to no one in particular).]

GEOFF   It's not *my* fault, is it? Somebody has to organize the family service for the church!

[Geoff stands and exits in the opposite direction to Veronica. Blackout. The discussion leader takes over.]

QUESTIONS

1. Clearly this is a family in conflict. What is the conflict? Is Geoff right or wrong? Is Veronica being unreasonable? Explain your answers.

2. Do you know people – either men or women – who seem to put things ahead of their families or relationships? Do you agree or disagree with their priorities? Explain your answer.

42. **The coat of many needles**

THEME
Self-indulgence.

SITUATION
In which we hear an unusual parable in the form of a Readers'
Theatre.

CHARACTERS
Reader One
Reader Two
Reader Three

PLACE
A stage.

SKIT

[Readers are already on stage.]

READER ONE   Once upon a time there was a man who bought a Coat made of many Needles. Though the Needles were sharp and made the Coat prickly to Wear, he liked how he looked in it.

READER TWO   Others agreed and, eventually, a small group of Needle Coat Wearers assembled to form a Club.

READER THREE   Wearing Needle Coats became fashionable for some. Others treated the practice with curiosity. Still others thought it was downright ridiculous.

READER ONE   "What's the point?"

READER THREE   The Non-Needle Coat Wearers asked without meaning to make a pun.

READER ONE   "Needle Coats don't keep you warm, they serve no specific purpose whatsoever, they appear to be painful and, frankly, defy good sense about Coat-Wearing."

READER TWO   Some communities, alarmed at such an improper use of Coats, made Needle Coats unlawful.

READER THREE   Feeling rebuked, Needle Coat Wearers retreated to the privacy of their homes and clubs to enjoy wearing their Needle Coats. In public, they wore Coats made of fabric over the Needle Coats. This practice didn't last long.

READER TWO   "We're living a lie," they said.

READER ONE   The Needle Coat Wearers met to discuss the dilemma. One said:

READER TWO   "We have the right to Wear our Needle Coats in public."

READER THREE   Another said:

READER TWO   "We should be *accepted* for Wearing Needle Coats."

READER ONE   Yet another said:

READER TWO   "Only narrow-minded bigoted people *don't* accept Needle Coats."

READER THREE   This resulted in a roar of agreed indignation.

READER TWO   "Perhaps others *want* to Wear Needle Coats but don't know how wonderful they are! We should be allowed to teach them in the town meetings and schools!"

READER ONE   Others even felt that they never had a choice about Wearing the Needle Coats at all – they were *born* to Wear them.

READER THREE   When the final vote was taken, it was decided that some affirmative action was needed.

READER TWO   A clever public relations campaign ensued. Needle Coat Wearers portrayed themselves as good, happy citizens who were simply misunderstood.

READER ONE   More militant Needle Coat Wearers insisted that they were being persecuted and deserved special protection under the law.

READER THREE   Well-meaning Non-Needle Coat communicators fought on their behalf as a matter of principle.

READER ONE   Still, many people scratched their heads and said that Needle Coats were ridiculous, served no specific purpose whatsoever, appeared just as painful as they always had and, frankly, seemed to defy good sense about Coat-Wearing.

READER TWO   The question "*Why* Wear them?" came up again and again but was effectively stifled by Needle Coat Wearers and their supporters who claimed that such a question was ignorant, bigoted and not worthy of answering.

READER ONE   They created statistics to show that there were more Needle Coat Wearers than anyone had ever imagined.

READER THREE   A few Non-Needle Coat Wearers formed coalitions to stop the Needle Coat Wearers.

READER ONE   "It's not proper Coat-Wearing!"

READER THREE   – they said.

READER TWO   The well-meaning communicators began to question the use of words like "proper". "What does 'proper' mean? Proper for one may not be proper for others. Shouldn't the decision about what is proper be left to the individual?"

READER ONE   In due course, laws were changed to eliminate any rules related to Coat-Wearing.

READER THREE   One day it was discovered that Needle Coats caused fatal skin infections. Many Needle Coat Wearers died. Non-Needle Coat Wearers felt badly for them, but could only shrug and say:

READER ONE   "What do you expect when you Wear a Coat made of Needles?"

READER TWO   Needle Coat Wearers were furious and accused the Non-Needle Coat Wearers of being insensitive and lacking in compassion.

READER THREE   They then insisted that it was the responsibility of society and the government to pay for the research to find a cure for the infections.

READER ONE   The Non-Needle Coat Wearers suggested that maybe Needle Coat Wearers should simply stop Wearing the Coats.

READER TWO   "How dare you make such a stupid suggestion?"

READER THREE   the Needle Coat Wearers shouted.

READER ONE   As a temporary solution, Needle Coat Wearers began putting thin shirts on between their skin and the Needle Coats in hopes of protecting themselves.

READER THREE   It didn't help.

READER ONE   The Needle Coat Wearers continued to fight for acceptance, for permission to teach about Needle Coat Wearing as a practice equal to wearing other kinds of Coats, and for special privileges under the law to protect their right to wear Needle Coats.

READER TWO   Eventually, other groups emerged made up of people Wearing Coats made of Razor Blades, Animal Teeth, Children's Fingernails, and Coffin Nails.

READER THREE   Even many of the Needle Coat Wearers were appalled by such groups.

READER ONE   But, since rules of proper Coat-Wearing were effectively removed from society, no one could object.

READER THREE   The few remaining Non-Needle Coat Wearers who objected were censored as bigots and driven out of the country.

READER TWO   And the rest lived happily ever after.

READER ONE   Well... those who lived.

[Exit. Blackout. The discussion leader takes over.]

QUESTIONS

1. How would you interpret this parable? Do you find parallels between the situation in the parable and our society? If so, where specifically?

2. If society were divided between the Needle Coat Wearers and the Non-Needle Coat Wearers, on which side would you fall? Please explain your answer?

3. Under what circumstances should a group of people be stopped from doing what they want to do?

4. Do you believe that, under certain circumstances, people are born to behave in a certain way, even if that way is against the norms of behaviour? Please explain your answer.

43. Quite a surprise

THEME
Sharing the faith.

SITUATION
Two co-workers chat about a change in their relationship – and what it means.

CHARACTERS
Rebecca
Lori

PLACE
Rebecca's living room.

SKIT

[Rebecca enters, followed by Lori.]

REBECCA   This is quite a surprise. Please... come in. Sit down.
           Do you want some tea or coffee?

LORI   No, thanks.

REBECCA   It's good to see you. It's been a while, huh?

LORI   Yeah. I don't get to your side of the building much.
           I've been meaning to call you... for lunch or
           something. Like we used to. I've been busy.

REBECCA   It was a lot easier to coordinate schedules when we
           were working in the same department. *[Playfully]* But
           now you're the big-shot director and you don't have
           time for us peons.

[Pause.]

REBECCA   Well, this is a surprise.

LORI   I don't want to waste your time.

REBECCA   Not at all.

LORI   It's funny, really.

REBECCA   Funny?

LORI   Strange. The way things have changed with you.

REBECCA   Yeah? Like what?

LORI   You probably don't realize how much people watch
           you.

REBECCA   Am I under investigation? What are you talking about?

LORI   Your life. It's been so strange watching you get into this... life of yours. Christianity, I guess.

REBECCA   Oh, that. Yeah. I figure if I could step outside myself, I'd think it was pretty strange, too. Downright confusing at times.

LORI   But it was such a big change. Do you remember all those afternoons we went to The Dog and Parrot? And Friday nights at The Terminal? You were out of your mind.

REBECCA   Out of control.

LORI   Now, it's so... so... *[Can't find the word]*

REBECCA   Strange.

LORI   Yeah. Then you suddenly stopped. Next thing I knew, you were reading a *Bible* in the cafeteria. A *Bible*, Rebecca? And Kenny said you were working harder at your job. He said you were easier to get along with. We took a vote and decided it was a phase. But it's lasted a long time. *[Pause]* This is hard for me.

REBECCA   What's wrong?

LORI   Nothing's wrong. It's just that I want to talk to you about it, but I don't know how. Everything seems so perfect for you now.

REBECCA   Are you kidding? Nothing's perfect. Have I given you the impression my life is perfect?

LORI   Not perfect, then. But... something different. I knew it was going to be like this. I don't know what I'm saying. You have something different from the rest of us. Not just the talk. My parents go to church all the time – and it's never changed them. But you...
           [Pause] I want whatever it is you have, Rebecca.

REBECCA   You make it sound like I should write you a
           prescription.

LORI   Can you?

REBECCA   No. I used to think so – but now I don't. It's never
           that easy.

LORI   Then what is it? What do you have?

REBECCA   *[Shrugs]* I'm a Christian, that's all. I believe in... see, I
           have this relationship with Jesus Christ.

LORI   *[Slowly]* All right... I want to know how I can have
           one, too.

REBECCA   Are you putting me on?

LORI   No. I want you to tell me. Will you do that for me?

REBECCA   *[Thoughtfully]* Yeah... I think I can do that.

[Exit. Blackout. The discussion leader takes over.]

QUESTIONS

1. When you hear the word "evangelism", what do you think
   of? By definition, what is evangelism?

2. Do you share your faith with those around you? If so, how?

3. What does the Bible say about evangelism? What does the
   Bible say about how to do it?

4. List at least three distinct ways that people can share their
   faith with others (more, if you can think of them)?

Adapted from A Work in Progress *by Paul McCusker.*

44. **The family room**

THEME
The significance of place.

SITUATION
A husband and wife make plans for their new house.

CHARACTERS
Chuck
Sue

PLACE
An empty room in a house.

SKIT

[Chuck and Sue enter – Sue peruses the room as Chuck speaks.]

CHUCK   What do you think so far? Did I make a good choice?

SUE   Yes, I think you did. It's a beautiful house. Surprisingly spacious.

CHUCK   Not bad for two days, huh? I must've looked at twenty houses. But when I saw this one, I knew you'd love it. You love it, right?

SUE   It's nice, yes.

CHUCK   Not *nice*, Sue. I want you to say that you *love* it. If you don't love it, then we could be in trouble.

SUE   What is this room supposed to be?

CHUCK   I don't know. I think they used it as a family room. I think I'll turn it into an office.

SUE   *[Thoughtfully]* A family room.

CHUCK   Yeah, you know – television, pool table, dart boards – whatever we want. But it's perfect as an office. I've always wanted my own office at home.

SUE   It's a little big to be just an office. Why don't we make it a family room, too?

CHUCK   Honey, my books alone –

SUE   *[Gestures left]* Along that wall.

CHUCK   The desk and computer?

SUE   *[Points left]* That corner.

CHUCK   Just a corner? What *is* this? I'll get more use out of it as an office than we will as a family room. It's just the two of us.

SUE   Think about it, Chuck. It'll be nice to have a room like this. Didn't you grow up with one room in the house to play in?

CHUCK   No. My mother always made us go outside or to our bedrooms – everything else was covered in plastic. She was neurotic that way. Besides, we have a front room. Do you want to go back in and look at the front room?

SUE   When I was growing up, our front room was for formal occasions.

CHUCK   What did you do – entertain heads of state? Sue, darling –

SUE   It's good to have one room for visitors and another room for the family. It's like the heart of the house. I've never had a family room before.

CHUCK   Precious… we've never *needed* one. It's just us.

SUE   For now. But in a few months…

CHUCK   That's right. Which is why I – *[Pause/Beat/Catches on]* A few months? What's supposed to happen in a few months?

SUE   Chuck, I'm pregnant.

CHUCK   *[Stunned, then:]* Pregnant! But… *how*? I mean… *[Pause/Beat/He is happy, perplexed]* Are you sure?

SUE   *[Smiles, nods]* Yes.

CHUCK   *[Laughs, unsure of what to do]* Well… congratulations! *[He embraces her, laughs, embraces her again]* This is

wonderful! *[Steps back from her]* I can't believe it. Okay.
Okay. So it'll be a family room. *[Beat]* Let me show
you the garage. It's just *perfect* for an office!

*[Arm around her, he leads her out... Blackout. The discussion leader
takes over.]*

QUESTIONS

1. Think of the places in your life that conjure up feelings of
   happiness. Where were they and why do you think of them
   fondly?

2. Think of the different places where you spend a lot of your
   time now. What kinds of emotion do they give you?
   Explain your answer.

3. This sketch presents a specific memorable moment in a
   specific place – one which this couple may well remember
   for the rest of their lives. Can you think of specific life-
   changing events and where you were when they happened?
   If you can, tell about them.

45. Busy Mum

THEME
Single parents.

SITUATION
A mother comes home from work to her child – and much-needed help.

CHARACTERS
Mother
Grandmother
Child (Daughter or Son) [not needed in the shorter Version 2]

PLACE
A family room.

NOTE
There are two versions of this sketch, one requiring a child actor, one not.

SKIT (VERSION ONE – MORE ADVENTUROUS)

[Child is sitting on the floor playing with some toys. Her mother enters from work, tired.]

MOTHER   Hello, Becky! *[Amend name if character played by a boy]*

[She gives child a kiss and sits down on the couch – very tired.]

CHILD   Hi, Momma.

MOTHER   Whatcha doin'?

CHILD   Playin'.

MOTHER   Where's Grandma?

CHILD   She's in the kitchen lookin' for some... some... y'know that medicine she takes when her head hurts?

MOTHER   Aspirin?

CHILD   No... she called it "whisky".

MOTHER   *[Sits up]* No.

CHILD   Yeah – Gran'ma said she could use a coupla shots after bein' with me all day. *[Beat]* Does that mean she's goin' to the doctor's house? To get shots?

MOTHER   No, Child. Grandma was only fooling you. *[Beat]* I think. *[Calling]* Mother!

CHILD   Oh.

GRANDMA   *[Off-stage]* Coming!

MOTHER   *[To child]* That's her way of being funny.

CHILD   Oh! Does that mean I should laugh out loud?

MOTHER   Maybe. We'll see when she comes in.

[Grandmother enters.]

GRANDMA   Ah. You're home.

MOTHER   Hello, Mum. Ummm, Becky is under the impression
             that you went out to the kitchen to get some
             whisky for your headache.

GRANDMA   To get some – ? *[Laughs]* Oh no. I was just joking.
             We saw a television commercial and – oh, good
             heavens. You know we don't keep liquor in this
             house. Your father doesn't drink it. And *I* certainly
             haven't started.

MOTHER   You need to be careful what you say around her.
             [Or him, if a boy]

GRANDMA   I suppose I will. I'm sorry. I forgot what it's like
             having little ones around. *[To child]* I'm sorry,
             Becky.

CHILD   How come?

GRANDMA   Because I was only joking about the whisky.

CHILD   I'm sorry, too, Gran'ma.

GRANDMA   You are?

CHILD   Yeah. I meant to laugh out loud and didn't know I
             was s'pposed to.

GRANDMA   That's all right, dear. *[She sits down on the couch,
             nearly as tired as her daughter]*

MOTHER   Was she *[or he]* a lot of trouble for you?

GRANDMA   Not really. She *or he* just has more energy than I do.
          I'd swear she *[or he]* knows how to be in three
          places at once.

MOTHER   Funny – that's what I used to think about *you*. You
          were everywhere at once and you had eyes in the
          back of your head.

GRANDMA   You were *supposed* to think that. It's the only
          advantage a mother has.

MOTHER   I'm a mother and *I* don't have it. By the time I get
          home from work, I can hardly be in *one* place with
          just these two eyes open.

CHILD   Gran'ma and Gran'pa are taking me to the zoo on
          Saturday!

MOTHER   They are?

GRANDMA   Your father doesn't know it yet, but I thought it
          would be a good idea. You didn't make plans, did
          you?

MOTHER   No, but I can't expect you to –

GRANDMA   You're exhausted. You need a day to go off by
          yourself – or with some of those friends of yours at
          church. It'll do you good.

MOTHER   But… *[Suddenly – whether from gratitude or depression,
          it isn't clear – she begins to cry]*

GRANDMA   *[Moves to comfort her]* No need for that.

MOTHER   But this isn't right. You and Dad do so much
          already.

GRANDMA   Nonsense.

MOTHER   You do! It's enough that you've had your own kids to raise, I never wanted you to raise *mine*, too.

GRANDMA   You can't help that. You have to work to make a living.

MOTHER   It wasn't supposed to happen like this.

GRANDMA   Of course not. But it did. Nothing any of us can do about that. Bob made up his mind to leave and that's just what he did. It's not your fault – and your father and I want to help any way we can. You know that.

MOTHER   I know.

GRANDMA   *[Pats her affectionately]* Now, dry those eyes and come into the kitchen. I'm fixing a roast for dinner and I don't want the gravy to burn.

MOTHER   You're not fixing dinner, too.

GRANDMA   Too late. You're going to tell me you have the energy? *[She moves to exit]*

MOTHER   It's more than I deserve, Mum.

GRANDMA   Don't be silly. It's only a roast. Come along, Becky. *[She guides Becky off]*

MOTHER   *[Follows]* This is more than *you* deserve, poor woman.

[Exits. Blackout. The discussion leader takes over.]

SKIT (VERSION TWO – BRIEFER)

[The floor is covered with children's playthings – blocks, colouring books, etc. Grandmother enters, begins picking up. Barbara enters – obviously from work. She is physically and emotionally exhausted and collapses on the chair.]

GRANDMA   Hello, Barbara.

MOTHER   Hi, Mum. Where's Nick?

GRANDMA   Still napping. I didn't get him to bed until late.

MOTHER   Was he much trouble today?

GRANDMA   *[Sitting, still holding toys]* Oh, not too bad, really. I forgot what it's like having little ones around. He has more energy than I do. I swear he knows how to be in three places at once.

MOTHER   Funny – that's what *I* used to think about *you*. You were everywhere at once and you had eyes in the back of your head.

GRANDMA   You were *supposed* to think that. It's the only advantage a mother has.

MOTHER   I'm a mother and *I* don't have it. By the time I get home from work, I can hardly be in *one* place with just these two eyes open.

GRANDMA   It's difficult, I know.

MOTHER   I got a call from Adrian's solicitor today. They want to set up a meeting to start the divorce proceedings. *[Beat]* It sounds so... clinical.

GRANDMA   He's really going through with it, then?

MOTHER   Yes. *[Sighs]* It's so hard to believe.

GRANDMA   When are you meeting with them?

MOTHER   Friday afternoon. *[Pause/Beat, Realizing]* Oh, I should –

GRANDMA   Don't think about it. Gran'ma and Gran'pa are taking Nick to the zoo on Friday afternoon. *[Chuckles]* Your father doesn't know it yet, but I thought it would be a good idea. And, after your meeting, I think you should have an evening off to yourself. Go out with some of those friends of yours at the church. It'll do you some good.

MOTHER   But I can't expect you to –

GRANDMA   Barbara, you're exhausted. I know what this is doing to you. Just leave Nick with us.

MOTHER   But… *[Suddenly – whether from gratitude or depression, it isn't clear – she edges towards a good cry]*

GRANDMA   *[Moves to comfort her]* No need for that.

MOTHER   But this isn't right. You and Dad do so much already.

GRANDMA   Nonsense.

MOTHER   You do! It's enough that you've had your own kids to raise, I never wanted you to raise *mine*, too.

GRANDMA   You can't help that. You have to work to make a living.

MOTHER   It wasn't supposed to happen like this.

GRANDMA   Of course not. But it did. *[Pats her affectionately]* Now, come into the kitchen. I'm fixing a roast for dinner and I don't want the gravy to burn. *[Stands]*

MOTHER   *[Stands, follows]* You're not fixing dinner, too.

GRANDMA   Too late.

MOTHER   It's too much. You do too much.

GRANDMA   That's ridiculous. What's a family for?

[Exit. Blackout. The discussion leader takes over.]

QUESTIONS

1. Do you know any single mothers or fathers? How do you imagine their lives?

2. This seems to be an age when families are breaking up more than ever. What affect does that have on the children?

3. As a result of the divorces and fractured relationships, many grandparents find themselves raising their children's children. What impact do you think that has on the grandparents? On the children?

4. What acts of compassion could we do to help single parents, their children or their grandparents?

46. **The secret**

THEME
The social stigma of faith.

SITUATION
Two friends confront another about her (or his) strange change in behaviour.

CHARACTERS
Mary
Ruth
Anne

Note: with minor adjustments, the genders of these characters can be changed.

PLACE
Could take place anywhere.

SKIT

[Mary and Anne enter with Ruth. They are clearly insisting she join them to sit down.]

MARY   All right, sit down.

RUTH   Sit down? Why?

ANNE   We're going to have a little chat.

RUTH   What's wrong?

MARY   That's our question.

RUTH   What?

ANNE   We want you to tell us what's wrong.

RUTH   What're you talking about?

MARY   Something's happened to you. I can't put my finger on it, but you've got something going on and I want you to tell us what it is.

RUTH   I honestly don't know what you mean.

ANNE   Yes you do. You've been really... I don't know... quiet. You don't join in like you used to. You're withdrawn.

RUTH   Withdrawn. You mean, depressed?

MARY   No – and that's what's weird. You're *not* depressed – or even upset or anything. It's like you're... happy. Like you've got a private joke that you're not telling anybody. So spill it.

RUTH   There's nothing to spill.

ANNE   There is. We have a right to know what's going on.

MARY   It's drugs. Is it drugs? 'Cause if it is –

RUTH   Nothing to do with drugs.

ANNE   Sex, right? You've got a boyfriend.

RUTH   No.

MARY   A girlfriend?

RUTH   No.

ANNE   It's a problem with your parents.

RUTH   No.

MARY   It's us, then. You don't like us any more. You've got new friends.

RUTH   No.

ANNE   Then what is it?

RUTH   Just leave me alone, all right?

MARY   Not a chance. You're not leaving here until you tell us.

RUTH   *[Pause, considers them, then decides…]* You can't tell anyone.

ANNE   Of course not.

MARY   Not a soul.

RUTH   You promise.

ANNE   Sure we promise.

MARY   On my mother's grave.

RUTH   Your mother is still alive.

MARY   On my grandmother's grave, then.

RUTH   You never liked her.

ANNE   Just tell us!

RUTH   All right... well... *[Looks around to make sure they're alone]* I'm a... a Christian.

MARY   A Christian?

ANNE   You mean, like, someone who goes to church and things like that?

RUTH   Yes.

MARY   *[Groans]* No.

RUTH   Yes.

ANNE   But that isn't possible. You can't be a Christian.

RUTH   Why not?

ANNE   Because it's... oh, I don't know where to begin.

MARY   It's so uncool.

ANNE   You're talking social suicide. You can kiss your life goodbye.

RUTH   Why? Who says?

MARY   Everybody knows it. If it wasn't – don't you think more people would be like that?

ANNE   I mean, churches aren't exactly bursting at the seams from people crowding in, if you know what I mean.

RUTH   My church is usually full.

MARY   Full of *what*? Huh? That's the question. Old people and one or two younger people who don't fit in anywhere else. Is that how you want to be known?

RUTH   I knew you wouldn't understand. That's why I haven't said anything.

ANNE   But why does it have to be *that*, of all things? Drugs, fine. Sex, great. A battle with your parents, terrific. But what are we supposed to do with you being a Christian? Have you thought of that? Did you stop for one minute to think of how it would affect *us*?

RUTH   Sure I did. I've even been praying about it. *[Covers mouth]* Oops. I'm sorry.

MARY   Oh, this is bad. This is really bad.

ANNE   Well, the answer is simple. You're going to have to give it up.

RUTH   What?

MARY   Whatever you agreed to – or signed – you've gotta tear it up, take it back, cancel the order.

RUTH   Not a chance.

ANNE   Why not?

RUTH   Because it's… it's what I want to do – what I *need* to do. This is about my life, my *real life*. I can't just walk away from it.

MARY   Sure you can.

RUTH   No I can't. It's like… I've got a relationship now. With God. It's new and exciting and… well, I'm not giving it up.

ANNE   Then you've made your choice.

RUTH   Yes.

MARY   It was nice knowing you.

ANNE   I hate to see someone with so much promise
        just... throw it away.

RUTH   But don't you want to know more about it? We've been
        friends for years. Aren't you even a little curious?

MARY   This is about priorities. I might be curious, but I'm not
        ready to give everything up for it. Let's go. *[Starts to
        leave]*

ANNE   *[Follows]* You're going to be sorry, you know. This
        changes *everything*.

RUTH   Yes, I know. *[Pause, after they go]* Isn't it wonderful?

*[She exits in the other direction. Blackout. The discussion leader
takes over.]*

QUESTIONS

1. How is Christianity perceived within your social circles?
    How do people in general react to those who become active
    with their faith?

2. If you are serious about your faith, describe how people
    have reacted to you when they find out. Have you ever
    been mocked, ridiculed or teased about your beliefs?

3. How do you think your life would change if you became
    overtly active in your Christianity?

47. War wear

THEME
Spiritual warfare.

SITUATION
A shopper looks for specific clothes to help with spiritual battles.

CHARACTERS
Adrian
Salesperson

PLACE
A large store.

SKIT

[Adrian is looking around the Harridges' store War Wear Department. A rather slick-looking salesperson approaches.]

SALESPERSON   Hello, may I help you?

ADRIAN   This is Harridge's War Wear Department?

SALESPERSON   Yes, sir.

ADRIAN   *[Pulls out folded newspaper ad]* I saw in your ad that you have a full range of clothes for war.

SALESPERSON   With an emphasis on *full range*. Our motto is "If it's wearable in War, we have it". *Guaranteed.* Are you going into areas of combat soon?

ADRIAN   We're in it now. *[As if looking at a rack of clothes]* Are all of your clothes this colour – greens and browns?

SALESPERSON   Those are *camouflage* colours. A very traditional look in uniforms. We have brighter colours – paisleys and a few primaries – but the wearers tend to have a higher mortality rate on the battlefield. Perhaps I could serve you best if I knew *where* you'll be engaged in combat.

ADRIAN   Where?

SALESPERSON   Yes, are you going to a desert climate or the jungle or –

ADRIAN   No, it's *here* – in our home and neighbourhood and church...

SALESPERSON   Ah! Urban warfare. For that we have a line of Gucci fatigues and Ralph Lauren campaign accessories. Very tasteful *and* comfortable.

ADRIAN   *[Impressed]* Really? Gucci?

SALESPERSON   Oh, yes! Let me go in the back and –

ADRIAN   *[Pulls out a piece of paper]* No, wait. Before you do that, I have a list.

SALESPERSON   A list? Even better. I like customers who *know* what they want.

ADRIAN   *[Hands him the list]* Here you are.

SALESPERSON   Wonderful. No doubt that we'll be able to outfit your whole fam – *[Looking at the list]* er, what is this? Some kind of joke?

ADRIAN   You said you have *everything* for modern warfare. Guaranteed.

SALESPERSON   But... but what does this mean: the "full armour of God" or "armour of light"?

ADRIAN   Either should work.

SALESPERSON   We have all makes – the latest from France, Saudi Arabia, East Los Angeles – but "armour of light"? Do you mean infra-red?

ADRIAN   No. Just what it says.

SALESPERSON   I may have to check the catalogue. *[Looks at list]* "Girdle of truth"? I'm sorry, but I'm aware of all manner of combat lingerie, but nothing in the name of Truth.

ADRIAN   That doesn't surprise me.

SALESPERSON   "The breastplate of righteousness". A bullet-proof vest of some sort?

ADRIAN   It'll have to be tougher than that. We'll be
                dealing with fiery missiles.

SALESPERSON   "The belt of faithfulness"... "gospel of peace
                shoes"... "helmet of salvation"...

ADRIAN   Don't tell me you don't have a helmet of
                salvation.

SALESPERSON   High-tech hats of all makes, but... I'm so
                embarrassed... I've never heard of this.

ADRIAN   How about a sword of the spirit?

SALESPERSON   Bayonets, sabres...

ADRIAN   Shield of faith?

SALESPERSON   Safety screens, riot control guards...

ADRIAN   I should have known.

SALESPERSON   Now, look, we have the *latest* and the *finest* in
                battle-wear, but *these* things... Just what kind of
                battle are you going into?

ADRIAN   I told you: we're in it already. It's a *spiritual*
                battle. It's very real and very deadly. And we
                need these items to fight properly.

SALESPERSON   *[Brightens up]* Spiritual battle? Why didn't you
                say so in the first place? You want our *Religious*
                Warfare department right around the corner.

ADRIAN   Are you sure? I'm not asking for clerical
                collars...

SALESPERSON   No, no – they have a full range of clothes for
                Righteousness: robes, loincloths, semi-automatic
                study Bibles, the works. I assure you, they'll
                have everything you need.

ADRIAN   Guaranteed?

SALESPERSON   Guaranteed.

ADRIAN   That's good enough for me.

[Adrian exits.]

SALESPERSON   I think I'm going to have to expand my
                inventory.

[Exits. Blackout. The discussion leader takes over.]

QUESTIONS

1. Read Romans 13:12 and Ephesians 6:10–18 in your Bible. What do you think the Apostle Paul is talking about in these verses?

2. Do you believe in the concept of spiritual warfare? If so, who is battling whom?

3. Are you aware of a spiritual battle in your own life? If so, please explain.

4. How can you equip yourself to battle those spiritual forces that desire to hurt you?

48. **Lunch in the park**

THEME
Theology.

SITUATION
In which a woman having lunch in the park gets caught in theological crossfire.

CHARACTERS
Charlene – woman who is trying to have a quiet lunch.
Jane – another lunch-goer.
Robyn – another lunch-goer.

PLACE
A park bench

SKIT

[A park bench. Charlene enters with her packed lunch and sits centre on the bench. She carefully opens the bag and begins a meticulous process of taking the contents out and placing on her lap.]

CHARLENE   Nothing like a quiet lunch in the park.

[She finishes unpacking her lunch, tucks a napkin into the top of her blouse, and begins a rather dramatic encounter with the first bite of her sandwich. But before she can take the first taste, Jane and Robyn enter from both sides – see her – see each other (respond with an unspoken dislike) – and sit down next to Charlene. Charlene tries to remain casual, nods and smiles at each of them. They smile at her, scowl at each other when she isn't looking.]

CHARLENE   It's a beautiful day. *[She bites into her sandwich.]*

JANE   Yes, it is.

ROBYN   An incredible day if you're living in the centre of obedience to God's will.

JANE   Still better when you know you have salvation no matter how you've sinned – or ever will sin.

ROBYN AND JANE   *[To Charlene]* Are you saved?

CHARLENE   *[Struggling to swallow]* Well... what do you mean?

ROBYN   Have you ever confessed with your mouth Jesus as *Lord* and entered into a life of obedience to Him through faith?

JANE   Have you ever accepted the free gift of salvation by faith in Jesus Christ?

CHARLENE	Umm...
ROBYN	Free, yes, but wholly dependent on daily submission and obedience.
JANE	That's a doctrine of salvation by *works*, dear. We are saved by the grace of God through *faith*, not by works.
ROBYN	But we must *work* out our salvation with fear and trembling as God works within us. That is why we're saved to begin with.
JANE	I'm *saved* because I believe that Jesus Christ died for my sins and through that sacrifice, makes me acceptable to God from that point forward – no matter what I do.
ROBYN	But if you don't *live* out that faith through works, then your faith is dead.
JANE	Your faith is dead anyway if you base it on human effort to secure God's approval. Our righteousness is as rags...
ROBYN	Our righteousness is as rags, but His will is to work through us. We're created to do good deeds.
JANE	But if you *don't* do good deeds all the time – if you fall into sin – you can still be saved.
ROBYN	Not if you continually practise in sin. If you fall away, you shame the cross and there is no second sacrifice for sins.
JANE	But you can't completely fall away. By accepting Jesus Christ, you've entered into a covenant with God – a covenant *He* has sealed and locked away! We can't undo it!

ROBYN	Covenant schmovenant. If you remain in sin, then you probably weren't saved to begin with.
JANE	And you're not in a place to judge. You can't know my heart!
ROBYN	I can know your heart by your actions! You mean to tell me if you grab this lady's sandwich and shove it in her face like this – *[She does it]* – I won't know the condition of your heart towards this woman?
JANE	I'm saying that, because I've entered into an unbreakable covenant, I can take this banana and shove it this way – *[She does it]* – and it doesn't affect my position with this person. It will only affect my fellowship with her. *[To Charlene]* You're upset with me, right?
CHARLENE	Uh huh.
JANE	But it doesn't affect my position with her. *[To Charlene]* I'm still sitting next to you, right?
CHARLENE	Unfortunately.
ROBYN	But, as a believer, my salvation will result in obedience. If God says not to dump yogurt on this woman's head and I do – *[She takes a spoonful and plops it on Charlene's head]* – then you could determine the state of my salvation based on my action.
JANE	A single action?
ROBYN	No – we all fall once or twice. But if I *continue* to do it – *[She dumps spoonful after spoonful on Charlene]* – then it's safe to say I may not be saved. I cannot use my salvation as an excuse to sin, I must *stop* sinning –

[Charlene nods in hearty agreement.]

JANE	And that's the most ridiculous thing I've ever heard. My salvation is entirely secure in the love of God and completely independent of these actions – *[Charlene is terror-stricken with what will happen next. Her feeling is justified as Jane begins to disassemble Charlene's lunch and cover her with it. Robyn joins in].*
ROBYN	These actions cannot be considered independent from who you are in Christ.
JANE	God does not love me nor forgive me any less because I'm doing this. *[To Charlene]* Does He?
CHARLENE	I don't know about *Him*, but...
ROBYN	He does not love you any less – but you must reconsider whether you've accepted the fullness of His salvation. You're talking about a cheap gospel.
JANE	And you're talking about a gospel no one can afford – a conditional one.
ROBYN	Cheap.
JANE	Conditional.
ROBYN	Cheap!
JANE	Conditional!

[Charlene begins to interject as they continue.]

CHARLENE	Hey... hey... hey!
ROBYN AND JANE	What?

CHARLENE   What if our salvation is predetermined by
                  God and we have nothing to do with it?

ROBYN AND JANE   *What?!?!*

[Jane and Robyn run screaming – in opposite directions – from the stage.]

CHARLENE   Gets them every time.

[She happily packs up her lunch and walks off. Blackout. The discussion leader takes over.]

QUESTIONS

1. This sketch seems to deal with many different things. One is effective evangelism. How effective were Jane and Robyn in their attempts to reach Charlene? Are there parallels between this sketch and Christians or churches who publicly argue their differences while trying to reach out to others in Christian love? How do you think they are perceived by those who don't know or understand differences among Christians?

2. Theologically, with whom would you most agree: Jane, Robyn or Charlene? Explain.

Inspired by Chuck Bolte, Jim Custer & the Jeremiah People of long ago.

49. The nice creed

THEME
Tolerance.

SITUATION
The Nicene Creed is updated to embrace tolerance.

CHARACTERS
Reader One
Reader Two
Reader Three

PLACE
The stage.

SKIT

[Readers are already on stage.]

ONE   We believe in one God –

TWO   Though we worship many: our Pop Idols and Celebrities, our belongings and our bank accounts, our Rights and Indulgences, our Pet Peeves and our Egocentricities, our Individuality and our desires.

ONE   The Father, the Almighty, maker of heaven and earth, of all that is, seen and unseen –

THREE   If, of course, we accept the theory of Intelligent Design over Darwinian Evolution.

ONE   We believe in one Lord, Jesus Christ, the only Son of God –

TWO   But "only" in the sense that He was the only one who went to Israel at that particular time with that particular message; we mean no offence to the prophets of other countries at other times...

ONE   Eternally begotten of the Father –

THREE   Like Buddha, for instance...

ONE   God from God –

THREE   Or Mohammed...

ONE   Light from Light –

TWO   Or Confucius...

ONE   True God from true God –

THREE   Or Krishna...

ONE   Begotten, not made, of one Being with the Father.

TWO   Lao Tse, the Jinas, and the Shri Guru Nanak Dev Ji...

ONE   Through Him all things were made.

THREE Along with many other notable faiths and their leaders.

ONE   For us and for our salvation He came down from
       heaven:

TWO   Or *they* did.

ONE   By the power of the Holy Spirit He became incarnate
       from the Virgin Mary, and was made man.

THREE Figuratively, symbolically or rhetorically – it's not
       important.

ONE   For our sake He was crucified under Pontius Pilate –

TWO   For his revolutionary cause of peace.

ONE   He suffered death and was buried.

THREE Another great man killed for a great cause.

ONE   On the third day He rose again.

TWO   Transformed, transcended, reincarnated, reconstituted,
       of one with the earth. Or maybe he didn't. But his
       followers had to say so to support their wishful
       thinking and personal agendas because they couldn't
       cope with his death in the first place.

ONE   In accordance with the Scriptures –

THREE Well, certain interpretations of those Scriptures, which
       were written by men, after all.

ONE   He ascended into heaven and is seated at the right hand of the Father.

TWO   As is often said of the great figures of mythology.

ONE   He will come again in glory to judge the living and the dead, and His kingdom will have no end.

THREE   By "judge", we mean he will welcome everyone into heaven, no matter what. A God of love would never actually punish anyone for anything.

ONE   We believe in the Holy Spirit, the Lord, the giver of life, who proceeds from the Father and the Son.

TWO   Oh great Spirit of the sky, of the earth, the wind, the fire. Mother Creation. Collective spirit of all in the Cosmos. Us.

ONE   With the Father and the Son He is worshipped and glorified.

THREE   Not "he" exactly, since that would be exclusive to all the "shes" who also want to join us.

ONE   He has spoken through the Prophets.

TWO   In many ways, in many voices, in many forms.

ONE   We believe in one holy catholic and apostolic Church.

THREE   Or assembly of all believers of anything, collectively or individually.

ONE   We acknowledge one baptism for the forgiveness of sins.

TWO   Figuratively speaking, of course, allowing that by "sins" we mean anything we do that might unintentionally hurt ourselves, someone else or Mother Earth.

ONE   We look for the resurrection of the dead –

THREE   In all the aforementioned ways, literally, figuratively
         and symbolically.

ONE   And the life of the world to come.

TWO   In whatever form that may be.

ONE   Amen.

TWO   Amen.

THREE   So be it.

TWO   Shalom.

THREE   Aloha.

TWO   Ciao.

THREE   Have a nice day.

[Exit. Blackout. The discussion leader takes over.]

QUESTIONS

1. React to this sketch. Do you agree or disagree with the
   "reinterpretation" of the Nicene Creed?

2. There is a lot of pressure on the church to become more
   modern and update along so-called politically correct,
   inclusive and tolerant ways. Do you agree or disagree with
   that pressure? In what way/s do you think the church
   should change? In what way/s should it stick with its
   traditions?

3. What sort of criteria should the church use for change?
   Explain your answer.

50. Therapy

THEME
The value of professional counsellors.

SITUATION
A man visits his therapist for help.

CHARACTERS
John
Bob

PLACE
A therapist's office.

SKIT

[A few chairs to serve as an office chair and a couch. Bob enters and sits down on the "couch". He waits patiently. Then John enters, looks at Bob with surprise.]

JOHN   Who are you? What are you doing here?

BOB   The secretary outside said you'd be here.

JOHN   She did, eh? I'm going to have to talk to her about that. She was hired to do random nailfiling, not send strangers in off the street.

BOB   But we have an appointment.

JOHN   Oh. Of course. *[Pause/Beat]* What kind of appointment?

BOB   Counselling, right? That's what we're here for? You *are* Heathenbottom?

JOHN   Do I *look* like a Heathenbottom?

BOB   Frankly I've never seen one before…

JOHN   *[Pulls a notepad out of his back pocket and begins writing in it]* I can tell immediately that you're in a state of anxiety brought on by self-doubt and a complete lack of experience. It's a difficult world we live in, my friend. Change. Too much change. Falls out of my pocket when I get in and out of the car. But spend some time with me and all your troubles will be taken care of. *[He sits down]*

BOB   I have to tell you right up front that I'm not real keen on this psychotherapy stuff.

JOHN   That makes two of us. But I had to do this or fix refrigerators with my father. Could never wear my trousers loose enough for that. What about you? What are you doing here?

BOB   My wife insisted.

JOHN   She did, did she? *[Writes in pad]* "Domination." *[Pause/Beat]* Are you often dominated by your wife?

BOB   No. She doesn't dominate me at all.

JOHN   Relax. Don't be so defensive. *[Writes in pad]* "Defensive." Why don't you have a seat?

BOB   I thought one of us was supposed to lay down.

JOHN   Are you crazy? *[Pause/Beat]* Oops. I didn't mean that. Male patients rarely lay down any more. Besides, you'd have to fold yourself in half to fit on these chairs. Just stay seated. Tell me: do you ever have dreams about... Greenland?

BOB   No.

JOHN   *[Thoughtfully]* Hmmm. Why not?

BOB   I have no idea.

JOHN   Well *I* do. What do you think it means?

BOB   I don't know. You should know better than me.

JOHN   Ah – now you're evading responsibility! *[Writes in pad]* "Puts off responsibility – displacement of blame."

BOB   What are you writing there? I'm not evading responsibility!

JOHN   You *should*! What's the matter with you anyway? Don't you want to succeed in life – in politics?

BOB   Politics! I don't have anything to do with politics.

JOHN   You'll never get a position in the government if you won't have anything to do with politics.

BOB   The government? Who said anything about the government?

JOHN   You don't want to work for the government?

BOB   No!

JOHN   Hmmm. *[Writes in pad]* "A complete absence of goals." *[Thoughtfully]* That's typical of a man in your condition.

BOB   My condition! What is my condition?

JOHN   Uh-uh-uh. We don't want to come to any premature conclusions. *[Pause/Beat]* Where did I put my spare straitjacket? *[Pause/Beat]* You're *sure* you don't dream about Greenland?

BOB   No! I mean, *yes* – I'm sure! Look, what does any of this have to do with our counselling?

JOHN   Don't you know? It's as plain as the nose on the receptionist's face. Did you see that schnozzola?

BOB   I didn't notice.

JOHN   She could rent it out for Olympic ski jumps.

BOB   Is this being billed by the minute or the hour?

JOHN   Ah! A preoccupation with money. *[Writes in pad]* "Ebenezer Scrooge." *[Pause/Beat]* I'll bet you're the sort of person who places all the currency in his wallet the same way up.

BOB   I don't even think about it. Why should I care how I put my money in my wallet?

JOHN   *[Writes in pad]* "Apathetic."

BOB   I'm not apathetic! Will you stop writing in that thing?

JOHN   Does this intimidate you?

BOB   Yes.

JOHN   *[Writes in pad]* "Easily intimidated."

BOB   I thought we were going to talk here.

JOHN   Oh, really? What did you think we were going to talk about?

BOB   I don't know. Life... families... change...

JOHN   Do you think they have anything to do with your problems?

BOB   What makes you think I have problems?

JOHN   *[Writing in pad]* "State of denial."

BOB   I am not!

JOHN   You are too!

BOB   I am not!

JOHN   You are too!

BOB   I am not, you... you *quack*!

JOHN   Resorting to name-calling now? *[Scribbles furiously in his pad]* Just as I suspected.

BOB   *[Immediately repentant]* I... I'm sorry. I didn't mean that.

(John continues to write. Bob's curiosity is peaked.)

BOB   What are you writing?

JOHN   None of your business.

BOB   It's about me, isn't it?

JOHN   I'm not telling.

BOB   That's not fair. Let me see.

JOHN   Next time bring your own pad. This is confidential.

BOB   But it has to do with me, right? Why can't I see what you're writing about me?

JOHN   I'm not allowed. It's in the Hippoplastic Oath.

BOB   Oh, come on. Just a peek.

JOHN   Forget it.

BOB   *[More threatening]* I want to see that notepad.

JOHN   No.

BOB   *[Reaches for it, gets hold of an end]* Yes! Hand it over!

[A tug-of-war ensues.]

JOHN   No!

BOB   Yes!

JOHN   No!

BOB   Yes!

[They go to the floor in the struggle. At a climactic moment, we hear an alarm – as in, clock – go off. They stop their struggle and stand up in a very civilized manner.]

BOB   That's it.

JOHN   Time's up already?

BOB   Yep. It's a shame. I thought we were about to have a real breakthrough.

JOHN   I'm getting a little old for this.

BOB   That's ridiculous. You're never too old to learn more about yourself.

JOHN   Remember you said that when they cart me away with a cardiac arrest.

BOB   I will.

JOHN   You won't tell your secretary what I said about her nose?

BOB   Of course not.

JOHN   Good. Well... thank you, doctor.

BOB   Thanks for coming by, Mr Heathenbottom. See you next week? I thought we could try some word association.

JOHN   I wouldn't miss it. *[He exits]*

BOB   Let's see... *[He takes out a notepad and glances at it, then moves to exit. Calls:]* Mrs Grant, you can send in the next patient!

[Blackout (Bob exits). The discussion leader takes over.]

QUESTION

1. What was this sketch about? What does it have to do with anything at all?

51. **The test drive**

THEME
Who you are versus what you own.

SITUATION
An old man evaluates a car.

CHARACTERS
Old man
Salesman

Note: with a few adjustments the genders of these characters could be changed.

PLACE
In a car.

▬▬▬

SKIT

[Two chairs on the stage serve as the car being discussed. An old man enters, looks around, then browses our "car". Salesman approaches.]

SALESMAN   Welcome to the Motorway Auto Emporium. May I help you?

OLD MAN   Well, I'm looking for a car – for my grandson Bobby – for his graduation.

SALESMAN   You're buying him a car? What a thoughtful gift.

OLD MAN   Generous, too. Money's no object here.

SALESMAN   That helps.

OLD MAN   I'm trying to make a point about the importance of a man's reputation and a car was just the thing –

SALESMAN   Hey, some would say that a car is a man's reputation. Like this beaut over here. The Miasma Sports Coupe X7J12 Deluxe with dual overhead cam, 16-valve, 250 horse-power engine. 5 speeds (and that's for reverse). This honey'll go 0–60 in 6.8 seconds. Instant facelift with those kinda g-forces. What do you think when you see this baby?

OLD MAN   Breaking the speed of light and killing twelve people along the way.

SALESMAN   Exactly! You look at this wonder machine and you think speed, power and a certain "jun-ay-say-kwa."

OLD MAN   What's that mean?

SALESMAN   It's French for "sexy". Your grandson'll have to fight 'em off with a stick.

OLD MAN   Who: French people?

SALESMAN   No – *women*. You know. They'll be like moths to the flame when he puts the top down and *cruises* this beast down the highway – the wind blowing through his hair –

OLD MAN   Scalp, actually. He has one of those short cuts.

SALESMAN   The wind blowing through his *scalp* then. I'm just saying that if you wanna do something for his reputation, this is the baby to do it. Get in.

OLD MAN   Okay. *[Sits down]*

SALESMAN   How's that, huh? You can feel the power even when its sitting still. The horses under that hood are chompin' at the bit to *fly*. Take a whiff.

OLD MAN   *[He breathes deep, then coughs]* Smells like the horses did more than fly.

SALESMAN   That's the smell of a great car – full leather interior. And this darling's got power windows, power door-locks, power glove compartment, power ashtray – the works.

OLD MAN   Very nice.

SALESMAN   This is what being a man's all about – er, what did you say your name is?

OLD MAN   Jonas.

SALESMAN   Jonas. Like the whale. I get it. Comfortable?

OLD MAN   My furniture at home isn't this nice. Is that a *mink* ashtray?

SALESMAN   Wait 'til you hear the engine. You could sleep on it and never know it's running.

OLD MAN   Really.

SALESMAN   It's a powerful car for a powerful man. And wait'll
             you see how it handles. Even in city traffic you get
             a sense of control. Isn't that what we want out of
             our cars – control? You're in charge with this
             machine. Your destiny waits, your fate stands before
             you with waiting arms like a... a... large waiting
             armed kind of thing.

OLD MAN   You have a way with words. I wish my grandson
             could see this thing.

SALESMAN   Me, too. People *respect* a man with a car like this.
             They look at him and think, "now *he's* going
             somewhere."

OLD MAN   Where?

SALESMAN   Wherever your grandson wants to go! This'll get
             him there. You just... wrap your hands around the
             steering wheel and take control of life itself.

OLD MAN   How much is it? – And no haggling. I hate to
             haggle. What's your best price?

SALESMAN   That's more like it. Uh – 63,000.

OLD MAN   63,000? That's an awful lot.

SALESMAN   I thought you said money was no object.

OLD MAN   It isn't. Especially since I don't have a lot of it. But I
             might have it when he graduates.

SALESMAN   Uh... when does he graduate?

OLD MAN   Oh – maybe four or five years.

SALESMAN   Four or five *years*! Then why are you looking now?

OLD MAN   See, he's got this idea that having a fast car will
           make him more of a man – give him power and
           control – and I wanna teach him that cars are just
           things, you know? And power and control are just
           make-believe.

SALESMAN   *[Groans]* I don't believe it.

OLD MAN   A man's reputation doesn't have anything to do
           with what you've got on the outside, but who you
           are on the inside. That's what counts. See, I want
           him to know that. And you've helped a lot. Thanks.
           Why don't you give me your card and I'll make sure
           you personally get the sale when I'm ready to buy.

SALESMAN   *[Groans, deflated]* Uh... I'm all out of cards.

OLD MAN   Just as well... I don't live in this town anyway.

SALESMAN   *[Groans]* Thanks for stopping by.

OLD MAN   My pleasure. Oh – and you might wanna do
           something about that mink ashtray. The animal
           rights people will be all over you when they find
           out about that.

SALESMAN   Thanks...

*[The old man exits. The salesman shakes his head and walks off
stage in the opposite direction. Blackout. The discussion leader takes
over.]*

QUESTIONS

1. The old man in the sketch equates the belief that having a fast car gives the false impression of having power and control. Do you agree or disagree? Explain your answer. The old man also argues that power and control are make-believe. Is he right or wrong? Explain.

2. Besides cars, what other things do people buy that might give them particular feelings? What kinds of feelings do you get from things that you buy?

3. The old man says: "A man's reputation doesn't have anything to do with what you've got on the outside, but who you are on the inside. That's what counts." Do you agree or disagree? Explain your answer.

With thanks to Jim Custer and Bob Hoose.

52. **Worship**

THEME
Hymns versus modern choruses.

SITUATION
An individual offers an opinion on the debate between traditional hymns and modern choruses.

CHARACTERS
Speaker (could be male or female).

PLACE
Anywhere.

━━━

SKIT

[Our speaker enters, carrying an old hymnal, and addresses the audience.]

SPEAKER   Hi. Y'know, I've been talking to a lot of people lately and I've been hearing that they're really confused. About God. About Christianity. About living as a disciple of Jesus. Well, personally, I don't understand what all the confusion is about. Once I was filled with the Spirit and felt His power – there was no reason to be confused. Everything became clear to me. *[Pause/Beat]* I believe any confusion is the result of denying the Spirit access into our lives – as we are now. As we *live* now. Let me ask you. How can God give us His ongoing revelation if we box Him into worn-out ideas and traditions? Worship, for example. I was looking through this old hymnal. Some of this stuff is okay, I guess. But listen... *[Reads]*

> *A mighty fortress is our God, a bulwark never failing*
> *Our helper He amid the flood of mortal ills prevailing*
> *For still our ancient foe, doth seek to work us woe*
> *His craft and pow'r are great,*
>   *and armed with cruel hate*
> *On earth is not his equal.*

Seriously now. I understand the mighty fortress part, but who knows what a bulwark is? Sounds like a bird. "Oh – what kind of bird is that?" "A bulwark, of course." "Maybe even a warbling bulwark." I'm sure they were good lyrics for their time, but – now? Have you ever tried to wave your arms in the air to a song like this? Or play a tambourine to it? I don't think so.

    I brought my own lyrics to a little chorus I wrote. Here they are:

> *Praise Him, Praise Him*
> *Praise Him, Praise Him*
> *Praise Him, Praise Him*

> *Praise Him, Praise Him*
> *Praise Him, Praise Him*
> *Praise Him, Praise Him*
> *Praise Him*
> *Praaaaaaiiiissse*

[Meaningful pause.]

> *Him.*

[Pause for the second verse.]

> *Love Him, Love Him*
> *Love Him, Love Him*
> *Love Him, Love Him*
> *Love Him, Love Him*
> *Love Him, Love Him*
> *Love Him, Love Him*
> *Love Him*
> *Loooooooooove*

[Meaningful pause.]

> *Him.*

[Pause.]

> *Serve Him, Serve Him*
> *Serve Him, Serve –*

Well, you have the idea. The Lord gave me those words last night while I was sleeping. Has that ever happened to you? It does when you're filled with the Spirit. I claimed them by faith. Don't you think they're better than a load of bulwarks?
Thank you.

[Exits. Blackout. The discussion leader takes over.]

QUESTIONS

1. What is the purpose of worship? What is the purpose of music in worship? Is worship – and its various components – a matter of personal preference, or is there a singular approach that is mandated by God?

2. Do you agree with our speaker or not?

3. Compare and contrast the lyrics of several traditional hymns with contemporary choruses. How do they compare? In what way/s are they different?

4. Which approach to music in worship do you personally prefer? Why?

5. Some churches are torn between some members who want more traditional music and other members who want more contemporary music in worship. What do you think is the answer for those churches?

Adapted from A Work in Progress *by Paul McCusker.*